SCOUT PIONEERING
Ol' Fashioned Outdoor Fun

Larry Green

SCOUT PIONEERING — Ol' Fashioned Outdoor Fun!

Copyright ©2017

Larry Green

ISBN-13: 978-1979963244

ISBN-10: 197996324X

Printed in the USA

SCOUT PIONEERING — Ol' Fashioned Outdoor Fun!

This book is dedicated to three Scout Pioneering legends. First, John Thurman, Camp Chief at Gilwell Park for over twenty-five years, who many see as the father of Scout Pioneering. Second, John Sweet, the Camp Chief's associate and the creative author of this book's namesake.

And of course, Adolph Peschke, my chief pioneering mentor, the author of the 1993 Pioneering Merit Badge Pamphlet, the design engineer for the pioneering action centers at six national jamborees, and the designer of numerous "Scout-size" pioneering projects. Featured throughout this book, which in this regard is something of an anthology, are many of Adolph's own descriptions and explanations for pioneering skills, and various assembly procedures.

SCOUT PIONEERING — Ol' Fashioned Outdoor Fun!

Floating Flagpole Overlooking the James C. Justice National Scout Camp

CONTENTS

Dedication, 3

Short Intro, 7

Why Pioneering, 11

How We Started, 15

Chapter 1: Stumbling Blocks, 19

Chapter 2: Ropes & Poles, 28

Chapter 3: Anchors, 38

Chapter 4: Skills, 49

- The Square Lashing, 52
- Half Hitches & Clove Hitch, 58
- Common Round Lashing, 64
- Tried & True Tripod Lashing, 66
- Misunderstood Shear Lashing, 72
- Double Floor Lashing, 79
- Butterfly Knot & Rope Tackle, 83
- Roundturn with Two Half Hitches, 89
- Versatile Draw Hitch, 91
- Essential Rolling Hitch, 95
- Dual Purpose Scaffold Hitch, 99
- Dependable Constrictor, 102
- Half Knot Round Lashing, 108
- Whipping Lashing Ropes, 111
- Optional Diagonal Lashing, 119

Chapter 5 - Activities 123

- Vertical Hitching Race, 125
- Horizontal Hitching Race, 127
- Joining Staves, 129
- Catch the Snapper, 131
- Scout Stave Flagpole Race, 133
- A-Frame Chariot Race, 135
- Crossing the Alligator Pit, 137
- Ladder Building Activity, 139
- Everyone on the Tripod, 141
- Reactor Transporter, 143
- Lift Seat Processional, 145
- Roman Chariot Race, 147
- Rope Tackle Tug of War, 149
- Scout Stave Launcher, 151
- Freestanding Flagpole, 154
- Snake Race, 156

SCOUT PIONEERING — Ol' Fashioned Outdoor Fun!

Chapter 6: Camp Gadgets, 159
- Hand Wash Station, 162
- Fire Bucket Holders, 168
- Scout Stave Camp Table, 171
- Scout Stave Dish Washing Rack, 175
- Tool Racks, 182
- Scout Stave Flagpole, 188
- Clothes Drying Rack, 191
- Freestanding Trash Bag, 197

Chapter 7: Safe Pioneering, 200

Chapter 8: Project Building, 206
- Double A-Frame Monkey Bridge, 210
- Double Tripod Chippewa Kitchen, 222
- Two Basic Subassemblies, 229
- - Trestle, 230
- - Walkways, 234
- Single A-Frame Bridge, 242
- Single Trestle Bridge, 247
- Single Lock Bridge, 253
- Camp Seesaw, 259
- Camp Swing, 269
- Swing Boat, 276
- Four Flag Gateway Tower, 284
- 14' Double Ladder Signal Tower, 295

Pioneering Program, 306
About the Author, 312

SHORT INTRO

There are many books about Scout Pioneering that bring to light various aspects of this broad field. Most noteworthy are those written by John Thurman, one of the three pioneering legends to whom this writing is dedicated.

A major focus of this book diverges from what's previously been written. Much of the material is offered from the perspective of how a modern-day unit can deliver a pioneering program that contributes to the goal of making meetings and outings fun with positive outcomes. Additionally, much of the book's intent is to serve as a resource and a reference—something of a how-to manual. In that light, readers should feel free to skip around.

Throughout its pages there are numerous pioneering-related photos capturing real Scouts in action from real troops. Most all were taken by the author during Scouting events over a period spanning twenty years. They're included in this book to help bring the text to life. In fact, there are so many catch action Scout Pioneering photos within these pages, this work can also be viewed as a unique picture book for enthusiasts of traditional Scouting.

Presently, the world is enmeshed in what can be referred to as the "digital age." Appropriately, this book contains lots of direct links to YouTube videos illustrating skills and activities. Most are featured on the BSA's Troop Program Resources website http://programresources.org. Readers are encouraged to access these! They're intended to vitalize the material, and towards that end, they are very effective.

The included *how-to videos* were created as an online supplement for the skills presented in the pioneering merit badge pamphlet. They do more than merely illustrate how to tie a specific pioneering knot or lashing—they also put the skill into perspective pertaining to *how it's used!* The *Scout meeting activity videos,* featuring various pioneering skill challenges, were created to enliven the BSA's objective: *to enable Scout leaders to have fun meetings with positive outcomes.* This book places emphasis on giving Scouts repeated opportunities to put acquired pioneering skills into action, in a fun and/or challenging way. Nowadays, more than ever, this is an important component of a Scouting program that keeps Scouts involved and coming back for more!

Eating Breakfast at Their Camp Table

SCOUT PIONEERING — Ol' Fashioned Outdoor Fun!

PIONEERING

WHY PIONEERING?

Off to one side of the trail leading to a Scoutcraft area at a council Boy Scout camp, the council president and I passed a Double A-Frame Monkey Bridge recently built by the pioneering merit badge class. The president's face lit up. "A monkey bridge! Everyone *loves* a monkey bridge!" His enthusiastic reaction was exactly what I wanted to hear.

As a kid in the 1960's, seeing gateways, towers, and bridges made out of poles and held together with ropes always gave me a boost. Loud and clear, with a resounding voice, these rustic-looking structures exclaimed, "Scouting happens here!"

Since the beginning, pioneering has remained one of Scouting's signature activities. Sure, most folks looking at Scouting from the outside, associate Scouts with helping little old ladies across the street and lighting fires by rubbing two sticks together. But to many, Scouting is synonymous with eye-catching pioneering structures. Over a hundred years after

Scouting's beginning, a young Scout yelled out, "Here's the stuff! Here's what I was looking for!" This was his exclamation as he entered the pioneering area at the national jamboree and caught a view of the wide array of bridges, towers, and catapults.

Amongst all the numerous outdoor activities in which Scouts engage, pioneering stands out in its scope for yielding the widest range of positive outcomes. Hand in hand with the actual building, and the fun inherent in the subsequent use of a sturdy bridge, dependable raft, elaborate camp gadget, or ingenious gateway, are the *opportunities* to gain useful skills, carefully plan things out, organize materials, and cooperatively work together as a team.

When a full-scale pioneering project is safely and effectively constructed, Scouts invariably enjoy a well-deserved sense of accomplishment. But, perhaps one of the main, underlying sources of satisfaction stems from the knowledge that the Scout skills they've acquired can be put into action in a fashion that is both practical and impressive.

WHY PIONEERING?

"Pioneering is practical and character-building: the two essential ingredients of any program material for Scouts." — Lord Baden-Powell

Jubilation!

HOW WE STARTED

SCOUT PIONEERING — Ol' Fashioned Outdoor Fun!

A LITTLE BACKGROUND

In the mid nineties, right around the time of the first printing of Adolph Peschke's pioneering merit badge pamphlet, I started a Boy Scout troop. The new troop's theme was to be "high adventure," and from the outset, our plan was to get to Philmont. Coupled with this was an emphasis on traditional Scoutcraft, and we used our outdoor skills during meetings and outings. Practice makes perfect, and in short order, our troop members became impressively adept. At our first district camporee, as we did on every camping trip, each patrol set up their own dining fly, over their own kitchen area—of course,

SCOUT PIONEERING — Ol' Fashioned Outdoor Fun!

using the prescribed knots. Eventually, a rather impressive array of gadgets would regularly adorn our campsites.

Left: Hand Wash Station / Middle: Tool Rack / Right: Clothes Dryer

Naturally, because of the positive outcomes and what it both represented and stood for, our troop was going to do pioneering, and to start, we were eager to build a monkey bridge! Our first move was to get hold of the pioneering merit badge pamphlet. Adolph's edition, which was current back then, was exactly what was needed!

I poured over the section presenting the double A-frame design, and also became fixated on the straightforward approach to lashing together two poles with the Mark II Square Lashing. Though it had been around for decades, I'd never seen this method before, and immediately took steps to introduce it to our Scouts.

A LITTLE BACKGROUND

The next move was to get materials. Everything in the pamphlet pointed to 1/4-inch manila rope, so we bought some. For instruction, troop activities, and camp gadgets, Scout staves were by far the best way to go, so naturally we purchased a supply. The spars we couldn't buy, but behind the house of one of our troop families was a dense pine forest. There we harvested the poles we'd need for the bridge. That was well over twenty years ago, and at the time of this writing, many of those original spars are still being used for a variety of activities (Chapter 5) and projects (Chapter 8)!

Early Monkey Bridge Built on a Camping Trip

SCOUT PIONEERING — Ol' Fashioned Outdoor Fun!

CHAPTER 1

SCOUT PIONEERING — Ol' Fashioned Outdoor Fun!

STUMBLING BLOCKS

"Determination remains the enduring answer to most problems." — John Thurman

Dutch Oven Cooking on a Chippewa Kitchen

We know with certainty that the majority of Scouts *do* like pioneering, and the better they get at it, the *more* they like it. So, if the Scouts have the desire, why aren't more Scout units providing the remarkable fun that goes hand in hand with building a wide range of pioneering structures?

The reason is obvious. Somewhere there's an obstacle. If there wasn't, more and more Scouts would be happily involved enjoying successful unit pioneering programs—building ever-more wonderful things at camp, on outings, and during camporees. If there's a desire to get involved in pioneering, then the simple solution is embodied in the quote by John Thurman that opened up this chapter. Where there's a will there's a way! The adventure, involvement, challenges, and fun are built right into Scout Pioneering—and also the success. And, nothing succeeds like success! So lets start right there.

NOTHING SUCCEEDS LIKE SUCCESS.

Generally speaking, experiencing failure is not a way to spark enthusiasm and rarely results in an exclamation like, "Hey! That was fun!"

Without the prerequisite skills, pioneering structures won't work or stay standing. That's no way to equate pioneering with something Scouts can feel successful doing, and that's no fun. But, just teaching Scouts the ropes is not enough! Unless the training sessions on knotting and lashing are "tied" to some fun or practical application, then repeated knot-tying and lashing sessions will become boring—an inevitable turn off. Not good! After introducing skills, give Scouts a real opportunity to put them into action!

Putting Skills into Action! (Scout Stave Launchers)

Each pioneering venture at a troop meeting or on an outing should match the Scouts' level of skill. That way, success is assured, and each new success is a building block to a bigger one. When these initial forays into pioneering are successfully carried out, then it's a sure bet that actually building the useful camp gadget and larger campsite improvement will have its own success story with a tangible outcome in the form of a concrete accomplishment. *"We built that!"*

IS THERE A LACK OF TRAINING?

It's entirely possible the troop leaders themselves don't possess the wherewithal to present the necessary skills and techniques required to construct even a simple camp gadget, not to mention a bridge.

This is no excuse. The basic knowledge and skills required are super easy to gain. There are plenty of knot and lashing diagrams and written instructions, how-to videos http://www.programresources.org/pioneering-skills/, and learning opportunities from experienced Scouts and Scouters. These resources are available to one and all. What it takes is devoting some time to mastering particular skills so they can be passed along directly to the Scouts, or to those who will be doing the instructing. Just like with pioneering materials, skills can be presented in accordance with those necessary to carry out the specific activity, meet the specific challenge, or build the chosen project.

DON'T HAVE THE MATERIALS?

Lack of equipment and materials is easily the most understandable of all deterrents. Naturally, when there are limited, or even zero materials, implementing a unit pioneering program can be daunting proposition. For smaller camp gadgets you can use broom sticks, Scout staves and binder twine. But, for larger projects, you need the right kind of lashing ropes and the right kinds of spars.

First, gather the materials needed based on where you are in the cumulative pioneering process. Begin with what's necessary for training and Scout meeting activities, and then add the components required for a chosen project. Start with the more simple, like a Double A-frame Monkey Bridge. That way, you can begin to develop your pioneering program around the specific project you've got in your sights.

Make an ongoing and concerted effort to get everyone on board to help locate and gather the materials needed to build the targeted project(s). This is a whole lot easier and more practical than having one individual assuming the responsibility all by himself.

Check with the owners of land where there are stands of trees that are good for making spars. Share with them what you want to do with the spars, and maybe even offer to do a little conservation-minded thinning out of some trees, which will be beneficial to the overall tree population. And again, start with what is needed. Expand as you go. Necessity is the mother of invention.

Team up with other Scouters in neighboring units, in the District or in the Council, and put together a pioneering kit for communal use. Remember, for a unit interested in putting together their own pioneering kit, a good place to start is to gather the materials necessary to undertake the specific project or projects the unit wishes to build. More supplies can be added to the unit's kit to meet additional demands for materials, as required by the desire and wherewithal to tackle new and different projects.

If you're in an area that just ain't got no trees, check into building a pioneering kit made up of laminated spars.

Additional information for laminated spars:
https://wp.me/p30vwr-jz

Utilizing a forked stick with the bail of an 8-quart pot, a Scout pours hot water into the third basin of his Scout Stave Dish Washing Rack.

"Greater efforts are obviously needed to open up this adventurous, creative, challenging Scouting activity to the Scouts who would undoubtedly revel in it if given the chance to do so. Everything, finally, will depend on the attitude of the troop's Scouters, and they are the

ones who must be won over. Scouters who are pioneering will need no encouragement and might even have to be restrained! To the others, we would merely say that in all fairness they should at least allow their Scouts to have a go. One thing is pretty certain. If they do, they will add another dimension to their training program." — John Sweet

Scouts cook their patrol's dinner in their outdoor kitchen filled with an array of pioneering camp gadgets.

CHAPTER 2

SCOUT PIONEERING — Ol' Fashioned Outdoor Fun!

ROPES & POLES

Fundamentally, Scout Pioneering is all about building structures using rope and poles. Getting a pioneering program underway requires a proper supply of these two essentials, for skills instruction, troop meeting activities, and pioneering projects.

ROPE

When lashing together poles for pioneering projects, the rope preferred is 1/4-inch manila. For applying square and round lashings to Scout staves, cut the rope into generous 6-foot lengths. We color-coded our 6-foot lashing ropes by dipping the ends in a bit of green paint. For applying tripod lashings to Scout staves, 10-foot lengths will work just fine. We color-coded the ends of our 10-footers white. The most common length for applying square lashings to pioneering structures is 15 feet. The tips of these lashing ropes were dipped in a little red paint. For thicker spars, and tripod lashings, 20 feet suffices—color-coded: blue. 50-foot lengths of manila have a variety of uses. We color-coded our 50-footers yellow.

What follows are some questions and answers about lashing ropes:

Where can I get manila rope? 1/4-inch manila is commonly available at a variety of large hardware and building supply stores. But don't be fooled. Make sure it's pure manila rope, made in the Philippines! For larger quantities, procure a box containing 1,200 feet from a reputable rope supplier.

Anything need to be done to the rope before its ready to use for skills instruction and building?
1. Though manila has a very low stretch value, put some strain on a long length, before cutting it into measured lashing ropes.

New ropes need to be stretched, before they are fit for use. One Scout only can do it! After the first stretch, the slack should be taken up and the process repeated once only.

Construction and Care of Rope, from *Scout Pioneering* by John Sweet

2. After cutting the rope into the desired lengths, whip the ends with a Sailmaker's or West Country whipping.

3. After the ropes have been whipped, color-code the tips by dipping the ends in a little paint.

4. Burn off any hairy fibers by touching them with a flame.

Can I just tape the ends? Sure, but that's not going to last long. Learn to tie a Sailmaker's or Half Knot Whipping so the ends don't unravel during use. The Half Knot Whipping is frequently preferred because it's easier to learn and apply.

Is there a reason we shouldn't hank lashing ropes? Winding tight wraps around coils of natural fiber rope results in leaving curls on the end performing the wraps. This makes the lashing process less smooth. To maintain their shape and for convenience, lashing ropes of the same length can be coiled together and secured with a short length of cord.

Coils of Manila Rope

Sized Coils of Manila Lashing Ropes in a Waterproof Bin

What's a good way to store lashing ropes? For easy access and portability, coils of lashing ropes can be stored in a waterproof container. Before storage, always make sure the ropes are completely dry.

POLES

Wooden poles are the main ingredient in building a pioneering structure. Depending on the project at hand, they're used in a variety of different lengths and diameters.

For instruction, procure a good supply of Scout staves—ideally, one for every Scout. The BSA supply division refers to these useful poles as Hiking Staffs. In addition to skills instruction, they're great for a variety of troop meeting activities and for building camp gadgets!

A Bundle of Scout Staves

Additional Scout stave information: https://scoutpioneering.com/2014/10/14/scout-staves/

What follows are some questions and answers about poles for Scout Pioneering:

What is a spar? In pioneering, a spar is a thick, strong pole. A pioneering project must be able to withstand the strain and stress that will occur while performing its intended function. We can't build a structure out of spindly sticks tied together with string and expect it to work. We use spars lashed together with good, natural fiber rope!

What kind of trees make good spars? Most anything growing in your area that is straight with a minimum of taper will work. Pine is widely used because it grows so straight and when stripped of its bark and dried out, it makes spars that are not too heavy and suitable for projects that are "Scout-size." Hardwoods can also be used and because of their strength, slightly smaller diameters can be selected to save on the weight.

Where do we get them? In most parts of the country, there are large, forested areas where, with the proper permission and clearance, you can harvest the spars you need. Most natural and planted stands require thinning at certain stages of their development in order to sustain good tree growth throughout the life of the stand. Thinning is beneficial to the overall health of a stand of trees.

What lengths and how thick? Depends on what you're building. Many Scout pioneering projects have plans that include a list of materials detailing the size of the spars you'll need. 6, 8, 10, and 12-foot lengths are the most commonly used for "Scout-size" projects. Diameters vary from 2 to 4 inches at the butt end.

Why is it good to remove the bark from spars? Stripping off the bark is advisable for three reasons:
1. If the bark gets loose under a lashing, the lashing can slip and cause the structure to rack.
2. Skinning the spars lengthens their life, keeping them freer from insects and rot.
3. Pioneering projects look nicer when spars are without bark.

ROPES & POLES

Twelve, Ten, Eight, and Six-foot Spars

Is a Scout stave a spar? No. By themselves, they're too skinny. Scout staves are great for instruction and small projects, but a 5-foot Scout Stave is a strong stick, not a spar. Many camp gadgets can be built using short, smaller diameter poles, like Scout staves.

Is a bamboo pole a spar? A bamboo pole is a bamboo pole. Large diameter bamboo is certainly thick, and depending on it's condition, also strong. However, it should be born in mind, bamboo can withstand vertical stress much better than horizontal stress. It's super for a variety of pioneering uses because it's wonderfully straight and for its size it's very lightweight. Due to its surface being so slick, lashing bamboo poles together can present additional challenges.

"Spar Barn"

ROPES & POLES

Where's a good place to store our poles? Anywhere out of the weather is fine, but it's often easier to store longer, heavier poles in a place erected just for that purpose. A "spar barn" is an easily accessible, outdoor structure that keeps the poles protected from rain, and at the same time provides ample air circulation.

View "Lashing Ropes and Spars" programresources.org/ropes-and-spars/

CHAPTER 3

ANCHORS

Tightening the Foot Rope between their 3-2-1 Anchor and the A-frames of their Monkey Bridge

Any pioneering project that cannot safely stand by itself needs to be attached to something that will securely hold it in place. It has to be anchored. Sometimes nature will provide a tree or rock in just the right location, or you might be able to shift the project's placement to take advantage of a natural anchor. On all other occasions, in order to assure the stability of the structure, anchors need to be built.

Stakes – When nature does not provide a solution, anchors can be built using strong pioneering stakes. The common size of stakes for most Scout Pioneering projects is

2-1/2-inches in diameter and about 24 to 30 inches long. After cutting the stake to this size, cut a point on one end. It's good to bevel the top edge to minimize mushrooming or splitting that can occur as the stake is driven into the ground. Long-lasting pioneering stakes are made of hardwood, such as oak or hickory.

Pioneering Stakes and Mallet

Drive the stakes into the ground at about a 20° angle. Soil conditions can vary and will dictate how large and long a stake you need. The main thing is to make sure all stakes are deep enough so they don't wobble or budge at all. *Under no*

ANCHORS

conditions should tent pegs be used for pioneering stakes. They're neither long enough or strong enough to make a safe anchor.

Taking Turns Driving in Pioneering Stakes

Mallet – When driving stakes into the ground, it's best to use a wooden mallet. Using a metal sledge hammer can more easily damage the stake. To make a wooden mallet, cut a 4-inch diameter piece of hardwood, such as hickory, elm, or sycamore, to about 11 inches in length. It should weigh about four pounds. Drill a 1-1/8 inch diameter hole to mount the handle. The handle can be made from a 24 inch length of hardwood (similar to making a stake). Use a knife or ax to round the end of the handle to fit the hole in the mallet head. Secure the handle in place with a wedge placed crosswise to the length of the head.

Though it's hard work, Scouts *love* to swing a mallet. For safety, and to preserve the stakes, they must remember to do it carefully!

Guylines – When attaching a guyline, make sure its contact with the stake is as low to the ground as possible. If the guyline is positioned higher or slips, it's likely there will be enough leverage to pull the stake loose. Guylines should be secured to the structure about 3/4 of the way up. To determine how long a guyline should be, measure the height at the point where its attached and double that distance. That's how far away the anchor should be from the pole. For example, if the guyline is attached 10 feet up the pole, the anchor should be a minimum of 20 feet from the base.

3-2-1 Anchor – As the name implies, the 3-2-1 anchor is made by driving stakes in a series: three stakes, then two stakes, and then one stake to form the anchor. First drive in the set of three stakes. Next drive in the set of two stakes about 24

ANCHORS

inches away from the first set. Finally, drive a single stake in the ground about 12 inches from the two-stake set.

3-2-1 Anchor

Connect the stakes by tying a rope from the top of the three-stake set to the bottom of the two stake set, and from the top of the two stake set to the bottom of the single stake. Use at least two loops of 1/4 inch manila rope, or six to eight loops of binder twine. Then twist the rope tight using a small stick as a tourniquet. After the rope is twisted tight, push the end of the stick in the ground to keep it from unwinding.

Depending on the strain the anchors need to withstand, other configurations can be used, such as 2-1-1, 1-1-1, or even 1-1 for a lighter strain.

Log-and-Stake Anchor

Log-and-Stake Anchor – This type of anchor is easy to make and can hold a considerable amount of pull. You can tie the line directly to the log, or you can use a ring with a rope grommet as shown in the photo. To make the log-and-stake anchor, place a log 4 to 6 inches in diameter perpendicular to the pull of the line. Then drive in four large stakes in front of

ANCHORS

the log. Next, slip the rope grommet through the ring and then slip the ends of the grommet around the log. Drive a second row of stakes 24 inches behind the front stakes. Anchor the front stakes to the rear stakes with tourniquets made of binder twine or rope.

When building anchors, always be sure they are in direct alignment with the strain being applied.

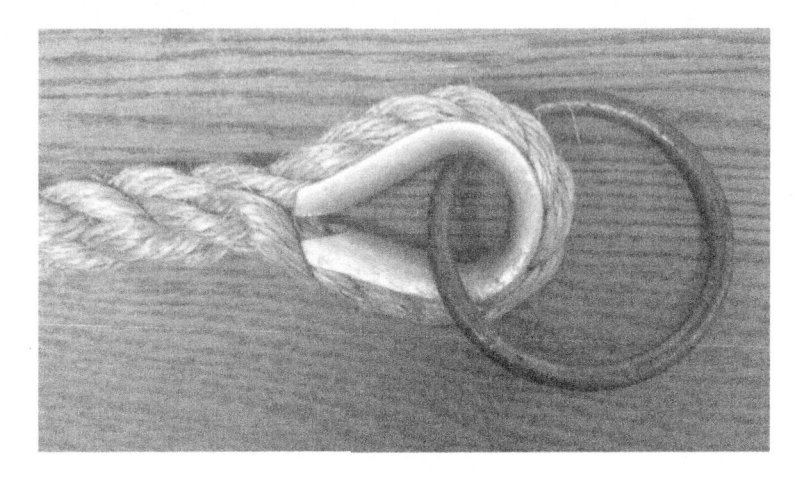

Strop with Thimble and Ring

Strops – If you'll be attaching lines to a natural anchor such as a tree or large rock, a strop can be used very effectively. Splice a thimble with a large ring to a 10-15-foot length of 1/2-inch diameter manila or polypropylene rope. A piece of canvas or burlap should be used to protect the rope from sharp edges of a rock or to protect the bark of the tree from rope burns.

View "How to Tie an Eye Splice" http://www.programresources.org/eye-splice/

Rope Grommets

Rope Grommets – Rope grommets are useful when attaching a long line to an anchor of stakes. A large grommet can be made by splicing together the ends of a 10-foot length of 1/2-inch polypropylene or manila rope. If you don't have a spliced grommet in your pioneering kit, tie the ends of the rope with a Carrick Bend. Be sure to secure the ends. To avoid

ANCHORS

creating a weak link in the chain between the structure and the anchor, the grommets you use must be made of a larger-diameter rope than the lines they're connecting.

View "How to Tie a Short Splice" http://www.programresources.org/short-splice/

Rope grommets can be used for a variety of applications. With the configuration depicted in the above photo, a large ring connects the three ropes from a monkey bridge (left) to a rope that is reeved back and forth between that large ring and the ring of a rope grommet (right). The rope grommet, in turn, is attached to the anchor. Additional information is available on this Single Pull, 2-Ring, Anchor Configuration: https://wp.me/p30vwr-1TD.

View "Anchors for Pioneering Projects" http://www.programresources.org/pioneering-anchors/

CHAPTER 4

SKILLS

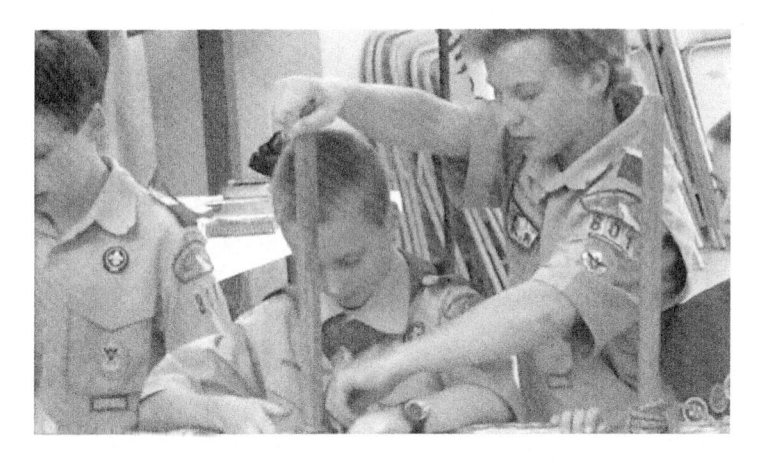

"There's only one activity in my experience where it pays to start at the top, and that is swimming. It is true that pioneering has often been directly or unexpectedly linked with swimming (as in raft building or bridging a stream) but, if any patrol, troop, or Scouter tries to start pioneering before establishing a sound background of basic Scout training in knotting and lashing, then pioneering will become unpopular and go down in the history of that patrol or troop as a failure." — John Thurman

In an amusing way, John Thurman is admonishing us. Before Scouts actually start *doing* pioneering, they need to become well-acquainted with effective, time-tested ways to use the materials! When presenting pioneering skills, always endeavor to tie the instruction to a relevant activity that relies upon actually using the skill. For that matter, this should be the standard for any type of troop meeting skills instruction. Even if the motivation is to just pass off some Scoutcraft-related advancement requirement, Scouts should be given the opportunity to use the skill! Putting skills into action bring them to life. It gives Scouts a do-it-yourself opportunity to gain a clearer perspective of exactly what the skill is for.

Putting Skills into Action! (Everyone on the Tripod Challenge)

SKILLS

In Scout Pioneering, a skill is presented because it will be needed for an activity that will follow in the immediate future —a challenge at a Scout meeting, or something on a larger scale. So, once Scouts are enabled to apply a pioneering knot, tie a lashing, or attach a guyline to an anchor point, they should be assured that what lies ahead is an engaging opportunity to do something with it, preferably in the same time frame as the instruction, whether during that meeting or on an outing. Something fun!

Note: There are numerous pioneering skills! The particular ones featured in this chapter were selected because they've been found to be so useable, and so frequently come into play. Of course, as long as alternative knots, lashings, and techniques safely achieve the same or even better results, there can be no reason not to put them to good use!

- The Square Lashing -

Before presenting the Mark II Square Lashing, let's start with the Square Knot. For years, Scouts have been taught to tie a Square Knot to join together two lines. Happily, at the time of this writing, it has become more widely espoused that a Square Knot is in actuality a binding knot. It's used to tie up parcels, close the flaps of a wall tent at Scout camp, as a first aid knot to secure a bandage around a part of the body, and when applied with slippery ends, used to tie down the laces of our shoes.

In Scout Pioneering, the Square Knot is in constant use. Mainly, it completes a Mark II Square Lashing. A Square Knot is also used to finish a Half Knot (West Country) Whipping, and a Sailmaker's Whipping. Additionally, a Square Knot binds

SKILLS: Square Lashing

both ends of a line down onto a pole, as when applying a simple strop lashing.

It's been found that the usual method of teaching a Square Knot can be greatly supplemented by introducing Scouts to what can simply be viewed as a *visual* approach. Actually *seeing* how the ends are positioned after the first half knot, enables the Scout to always complete the second half knot correctly. This is a good way to avoid the notorious granny knot, which can be more difficult to untie.

Visual Approach" to Tying a Square Knot ("How to Always Tie a Square Knot Right")

View "How to Always Tie a Square Knot Right" http://www.programresources.org/square-knot-visual-approach/

Mark II Square Lashing – This square lashing can aptly be named a "Square Knot Square Lashing" as opposed to what some consider the traditional approach to tying a square lashing by starting and ending with a Clove Hitch, (which can aptly be

SCOUT PIONEERING — Ol' Fashioned Outdoor Fun!

referred to as a "Clove Hitch Square Lashing"). James Keller, director of the pioneering area during the 2013 and 2017 national jamborees, related a story about the Mark II Square Lashing. He described how back in 1993, Adolph Peschke had

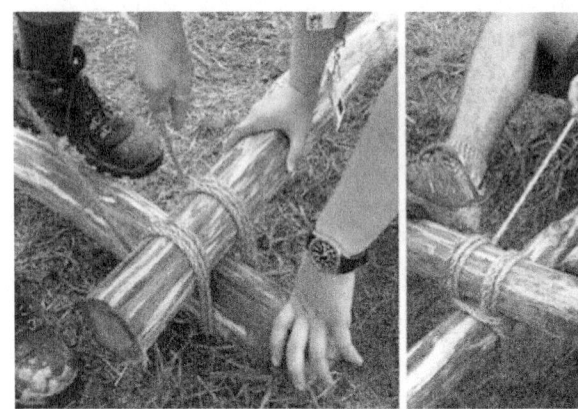

Mark II Square Lashing

mandated that the entire staff in the pioneering action centers of the national jamboree should just use the Mark II Square Lashing. Some of the pioneering staff back then had not as of yet become familiar with the lashing, and at first, they were a little hesitant to adopt it. But, you *can* teach old dogs a new trick! After becoming acquainted, their overwhelming consensus was, why had they wasted so much time over the years using the approach that starts and ends with a Clove Hitch.

SKILLS: Square Lashing

"The Japanese Mark II Square Lashing has found its way into Scouting in the United States through Wood Badge training in England, and because of the work of John Thurman, camp chief of Gilwell. He observed it on one of his many world trips related to Wood Badge training." — *Adolph Peschke*

Because this approach is easily twice as fast, more simple to learn, and has the same holding power as beginning with a Clove Hitch and then working only one end of the line at a time before ending with another Clove Hitch, the Mark II Square Lashing is a natural shoo-in with Scouts. The fact is, with this lashing, projects are built more quickly and with less tedium. The outcome is, Scouts are happily inclined to lash more stuff together!

1. Begin by placing the poles in the desired position. Fold the lashing rope in half and place the midpoint of the rope around the vertical pole just under the crossing pole.

2. Carry both ends of the rope up over the crossing pole and cross them behind the vertical pole.

SCOUT PIONEERING — Ol' Fashioned Outdoor Fun!

3. Bring both ends back to the front, carrying them down over the crossing pole.

4. Cross them behind the vertical pole, this time underneath the crossing pole. Continue this process forming three wraps.

5. After the third wrap, bring the ends of the rope back to the front and begin the fraps by crossing them in front of the vertical pole.

6. Carry both ends of the rope around the wraps, between the poles two times in opposite directions, and finish with a Square Knot.

SKILLS: Square Lashing

Building an A-Frame Bridge at the jamboree, three Scouts lash the transom and ledger to a pair of shear legs with Mark II Square Lashings.

View "How to Tie a Mark II Square Lashing" http://www.programresources.org/square-lashing/

- Half Hitches & Clove Hitch -

Applying half hitches around a pole with relaxed ease and confidence is fundamental and one of the most *useful* knacks a Scout can possess. What a quick, easy, and effective way to complete any lashing that's finished with a Clove Hitch, and snug it up tight against the wrappings! When it comes to the Clove Hitch, you've got to love John Thurman's perspective.

> *"The first and everlasting thing to remember about the Clove Hitch is that it is composed of two half hitches. What a very obvious thing to say, but there is hardly one Scout in a hundred who learns what it means. If only we can get Scouts to learn that if you make one half hitch and another half hitch and bring them together they make a Clove Hitch, what a lot of time the Movement*

SKILLS: Half Hitches & Clove Hitch

would save in the amount of fiddling and fumbling that goes on when a Clove Hitch is the order of the day. We would be able to start in the sure knowledge that we can make Clove Hitches and pass quickly on to better and brighter things." — John Thurman

First Half Hitch	2nd Half Hitch
First Half Hitch	2nd Half Hitch

Whether the line is proceeding from the right or from the left, Scouts should quickly be able to tie on half hitches without fussing around.

SCOUT PIONEERING — Ol' Fashioned Outdoor Fun!

Learning to tie a Clove Hitch in this manner makes much more sense than the customary, widespread approach of first making an "x" and then passing the running end through it. Trying to make room for the "x" when finishing a lashing can be confusing, not to mention difficult, when it comes to getting that Clove Hitch tied without leaving a space between the hitch and the wrappings. When a Scout is shown how to simply make a series of half hitches on a pole, both from the right and from the left, he will never have trouble tying Clove Hitches.

View "How to Tie Half Hitches to Finish Many Lashings"
http://www.programresources.org/half-hitches-and-lashings/

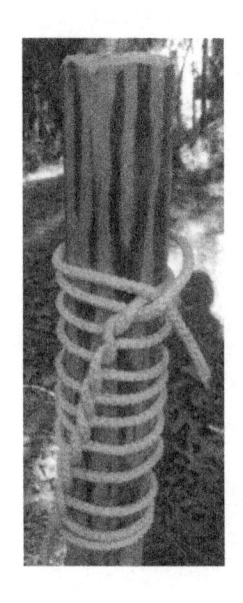

Then, of course, there's the Open-Ended Clove Hitch! Back in the 60's at Camp Wauwepex, a Scout camp on Long Island, one of the attractions in the Scoutcraft area was a vertical pole about 4 feet tall with a rope attached near the bottom. This was a "Hitching Post." It was put up so Scouts could see how many half hitches they could pass over the top of the pole as quickly as

SKILLS: Half Hitches & Clove Hitch

possible. Watching fellow Scouts who had mastered the simple technique provided enough motivation to learn how to do it too, and it was easy to get quite good at it. As we were "throwing" hitches over the pole with greater and greater alacrity, we weren't aware that every two of these hitches was a Clove Hitch. Nor would we have cared. It was just fun to see how fast we could get.

When preceding from the *left,* all that needs to be done is:
1. Form a right underhand loop https://scoutpioneering.com/2013/02/11/knot-tying-terminology/ and place it over the pole.
2. Form another right underhand loop and place it over the pole (on top of the pervious one).

When preceding from the *right*, instead of right underhand loops, form left underhand loops. This hitching technique is *very useful!*

- Securing a bag onto the upright sticks of a camp gadget designed to hold garbage bags
- Attaching lines to the upright poles of a tarp
- Tying a line onto uprights to fence off an axe yard

SCOUT PIONEERING — Ol' Fashioned Outdoor Fun!

- Attaching the hand ropes to the A-frames of a rope bridge

2 Underhand Loops = a Clove Hitch

It's really surprising how many folks, old and young, aren't familiar with this simple method of tying a Clove Hitch. Here's an amusing illustration: A young Scout was competing at a camporee for the best time in completing a Rope-Toss-Log-Lift Challenge https://wp.me/p30vwr-rh. After throwing the rope over the crossbar and tying the end to a log with a Timber Hitch, the third step is to secure the other end of the rope to a stake in the ground with a Clove Hitch. Ah! An open ended pole! So, this young Scout completes the first two steps, runs over to the stake and, bam! He ties a Clove Hitch over that stake in nothing flat. The jaw of the Scouter conducting the event drops down. With mouth open and a look of bewilderment on his face, he leans down, scratches his head, and examines the knot. Yes, to his surprise, indeed it's a Clove Hitch! This skinny,

SKILLS: Half Hitches & Clove Hitch

young Scout did something this adult Scouter had never seen before, and the old guy was astonished!

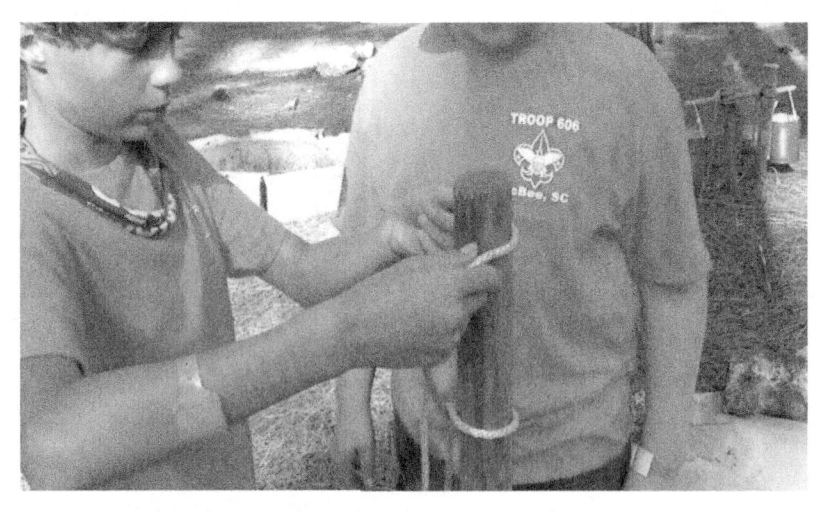

Scouts practice placing underhand loops on an open-ended, vertical pole.

View "How to Tie and Use the Clove Hitch and Half Hitches" Video http://www.programresources.org/half-hitches-and-clove-hitch-video/

63

- Common Round Lashing -

Two Scout Staves Joined Together with Round Lashings

A round lashing is most often used to combine two poles together to make a longer length that is as rigid as possible.

To tie this common round lashing, start with a Clove Hitch around both poles. Then take eight to ten tight wraps, again around both poles. Don't overlap any of these wraps and keep them flush against one another. End the lashing with another Clove Hitch around both poles. There are no frapping turns in a round lashing. The goal of the lashing is to join the parallel sections of the two poles tightly together. This is accomplished with the wraps. Applying fraps between the poles causes an unwanted and unnecessary gap!

SKILLS: Round Lashing

Joining two poles with round lashings requires a good overlap between them. Obviously, it also requires two lashings, each tied tightly, well near the ends of each pole.

Four Flagpoles Round Lashed to the Corners of a Camp Table

Scouting and flags go hand in hand. Patrol flags, troop flags, the American Flag, etc., etc., flags add color and engender pride. Attach flagpoles to the uprights of dining flies, to bridges, towers, gateways, you name it, with round lashings!

View "How to Tie a Round Lashing" http://www.programresources.org/round-lashing/

- Tried & True Tripod Lashing -

A bag hangs from three Scout staves lashed into a tripod.

Hands down, the most common of all little camping structures is made by lashing together three poles so they stand up by themselves. The notion of suspending a cooking pot over a fire by hanging it off the top of this basic and simplistic configuration seems to strike a romantic chord with the average camper. Perhaps because harnessing one's resources to fashion something useful away from modern conveniences resonates as an ingenious accomplishment. In pioneering, the tripod forms either the central framework or an essential subassembly for an array of neat camp gadgets and larger projects.

There are fundamentally two ways to take the wrapping turns. One, referred to as "plain turns," simply wraps the line

SKILLS: Tripod Lashing

around all three poles. The other, referred to as "racking turns," weaves the line alternately in and out between the poles. Plain turns are faster, and work well when the structure will remain standing for a shorter period. With racking turns, sometimes called a "figure of eight lashing," the line has more contact with the poles and therefore there's more friction and hence more stability. Either way, how stiff the tripod legs will be when they're separated depends on the number and tightness of these wrapping turns.

There are also fundamentally two ways to lay the poles when starting the tripod lashing: the butt ends of the two outside legs in one direction, and the middle leg with its butt end in the opposite direction, -or- all three poles with the butt ends on the same side at what will be the bottom. In most

67

SCOUT PIONEERING — Ol' Fashioned Outdoor Fun!

circles, the first way has all but been debunked, because it frequently results in forming the wraps either too tight or too loose. Therefore, in most all scenarios, start the tripod lashing with the but ends lined up evenly at the bottom.

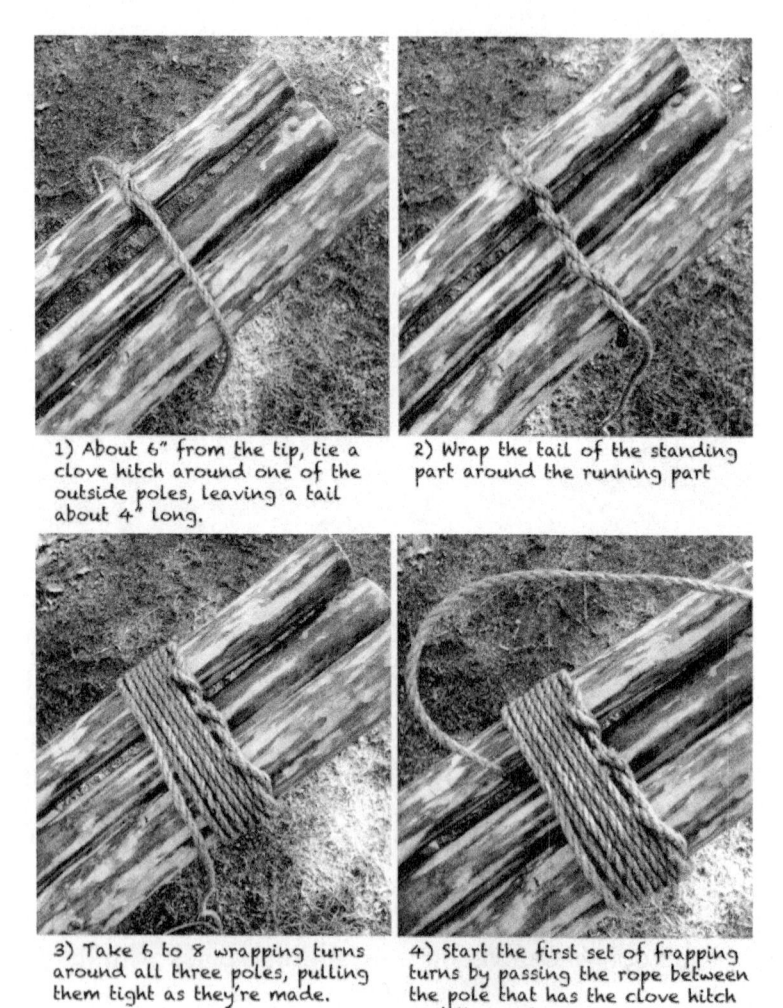

1) About 6" from the tip, tie a clove hitch around one of the outside poles, leaving a tail about 4" long.

2) Wrap the tail of the standing part around the running part

3) Take 6 to 8 wrapping turns around all three poles, pulling them tight as they're made.

4) Start the first set of frapping turns by passing the rope between the pole that has the clove hitch and the center pole.

SKILLS: Tripod Lashing

5) Take two frapping turns, pulling them tight.

6) Start the second set of frapping turns by carrying the rope over the middle pole and frapping between the middle pole and the other outside pole.

7) Take two frapping turns, pulling them tight.

8) After these frapping turns, carry the rope past the outside pole and then around it, forming the first of two half hitches.

SCOUT PIONEERING — Ol' Fashioned Outdoor Fun!

9) Work the half hitch tight against the wrappings.

10) Complete the clove hitch by tying a second half hitch and working it tight against the first.

Outside Legs Crossed Under the Middle Leg

When standing up the tripod, the outside legs cross *under* the middle leg. In that way, the strength of the tripod is not entirely dependent on the strength of the lashing rope, but also on the support given by the wood of the outside legs.

SKILLS: Tripod Lashing

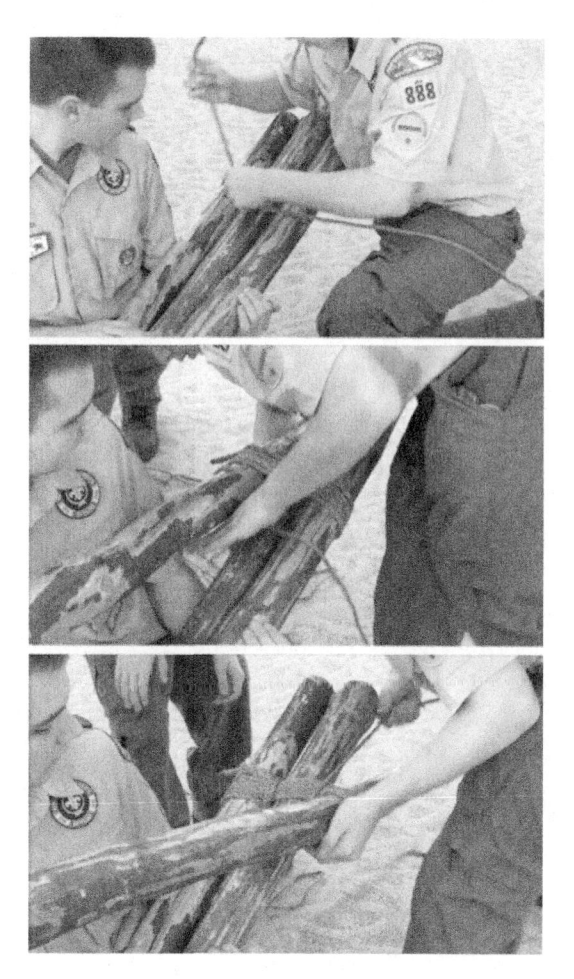

Scouts aid in the lashing process by supporting and lifting the outside legs, making it is easier to complete the frapping turns, and being extra careful not to pinch the lasher's fingers.

View "How to Tie a Tripod Lashing w/ Plain Turns"
http://www.programresources.org/tripod-lashing/

SCOUT PIONEERING — Ol' Fashioned Outdoor Fun!

- Misunderstood Shear Lashing -

A Shear Lashing Applied to Two Scout Staves

The shear lashing's *use* is quite clear. References to the lashing in John Thurman's pioneering books, in John Sweet's *Scout Pioneering*, and the pioneering merit badge Pamphlets by Adolph Peschke all describe its fundamental use exactly the same way.

SKILLS: Shear Lashing

Putting it neat like John Sweet: use a sheer lashing "when two spars are to be opened out like scissors to make a pair of sheerlegs," or right to the point like John Thurman in *Pioneering Projects*, the sheer lashing is "used for lashing together two parallel spars which will be opened out of the parallel to form sheerlegs."

What are sheerlegs? Sheerlegs (sheer legs, shear legs) are two upright spars lashed together at the tips with the butt ends splayed apart to support some kind of weight. Most always, in Scout Pioneering we use sheer legs to form an A-frame.

A square lashing provides more contact between the rope and poles, and hence more effectively joins the poles together. Therefore, when constructing A-frames, on occasion the shear lashing is not used at all. It is, however, easier to apply when the poles intersect at less that 45°, especially when the other ends of the poles are already lashed to other parts of the structure.

1. Place the poles parallel to one another and tie a Clove Hitch near the top of one.

2. Take six to eight wrapping turns around both poles.

SCOUT PIONEERING — Ol' Fashioned Outdoor Fun!

3. Make two complete frapping turns around the wraps between the poles.

4. Finish with a Clove Hitch around one pole.

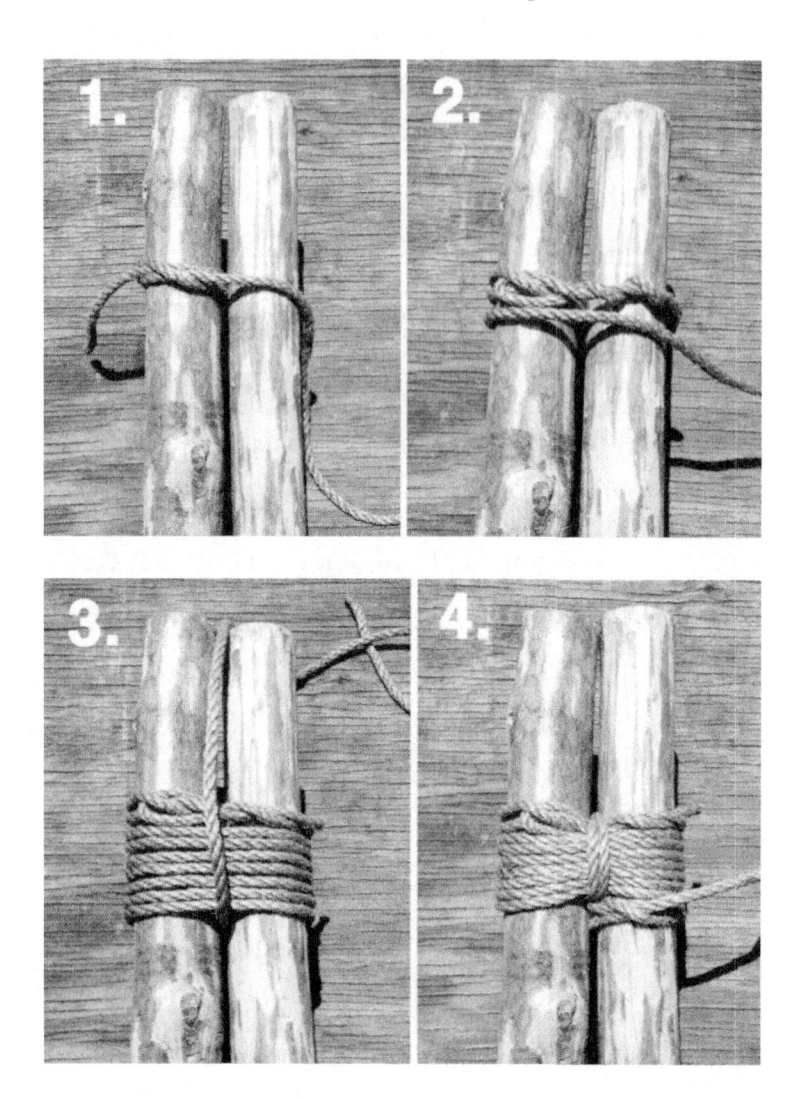

SKILLS: *Shear Lashing*

Left: Completed Shear Lashing / Right: Spars Spread into Shear Legs

View "How to Tie a Shear Lashing" http://www.programresources.org/shear-lashing/

The following is written in an attempt to provide some clarity and explanation regarding the inconsistencies that appear throughout various pioneering publications presenting the shear lashing.

Ambiguity in Labeling– Most modern references to the lashing spell it s-h-e-a-r. Yet, the much respected and revered

John Thurman was emphatic that the only correct spelling was s-h-e-**e**-r!

Let's take this opportunity to further clarify two lashing designations that keep popping up. A *shear lashing* is used to make shear legs. A *round lashing* is used to attach one pole to another in the same direction, as in extending the overall length of shorter poles. It can also be used to bind more than one pole together to make a stronger pole. *Shear lashings* incorporate frapping turns. Round lashings do not! Along these lines, the lashing referred to as the West Country Shear Lashing should be called the West Country *Round* Lashing, and rightfully so!

Nowhere is this stated more clearly than in Gerald Finley's book, *Rope Works*: "The West Country Round Lashing is also called West Country Shear Lashing, but this name contributes to the confusion caused by lumping shear and round lashings together. The West Country Round Lashing is used to form a rigid joint between two parallel poles; it does not form the flexible joint of a shear lashing and it has no frapping turns."

What is a Two-Spar Shear Lashing? More wordiness coming up! To add to the possible confusion, Adolph Peschke

SKILLS: Shear Lashing

calls what John Thurman refers to as the Sheer Lashing Mark I, the Two-Spar Shear Lashing. This name can also be related to the tying of our Tripod Lashing with Plain Turns, because the procedure is exactly like the Two-Spar Shear Lashing but with three spars. It follows that it's easy to dub this tried and true form of tripod lashing the *Three*-Spar Shear Lashing. The Two-Spar Shear Lashing is used to make an A-Frame, and the Three-Spar Shear Lashing is used to make a simple tripod.

Ambiguity in Tying the Lashing – Though the formation is the same: Clove Hitch around one spar, six to eight wraps, two fraps, finish with Clove Hitch around one spar, there are varied approaches to actually tying the shear lashing. These discrepancies all hinge on the "hinge." The spars have to pivot in order to spread out the desired distance. How can this be accomplished so the lashing is tight but not so tight that when spreading the legs into position, the legs and lashing rope resist the strain to the point that something breaks? The tighter the wraps, and the more wrapping turns you take, the stiffer the lashing will be.

One view is to make the wraps and fraps on the loose side, concluding they'll tighten when the legs are spread.

Another view is to place a small block of wood between the spars to yield adequate room for the frapping turns. Yet another view is to make the wraps moderately tight and then before frapping, spread the legs a bit to allow room for the frapping turns, *being careful not to close the spars on the lasher's fingers!* Finally, some like to complete the wraps, then spread the legs to the desired width, and then take tight frapping turns.

In addition to your personal preferences, whatever works well will also depend on the circumstances, the diameter of the spars, how straight they are, and indeed on the structure itself.

Scouts begin to tie a shear lashing to build an A-frame.

SKILLS

- Double Floor Lashing -

This is an effective approach to lashing on a platform, for a deck, table, bench, chair, or a Chippewa kitchen! When you get the knack, it's quick and easy!

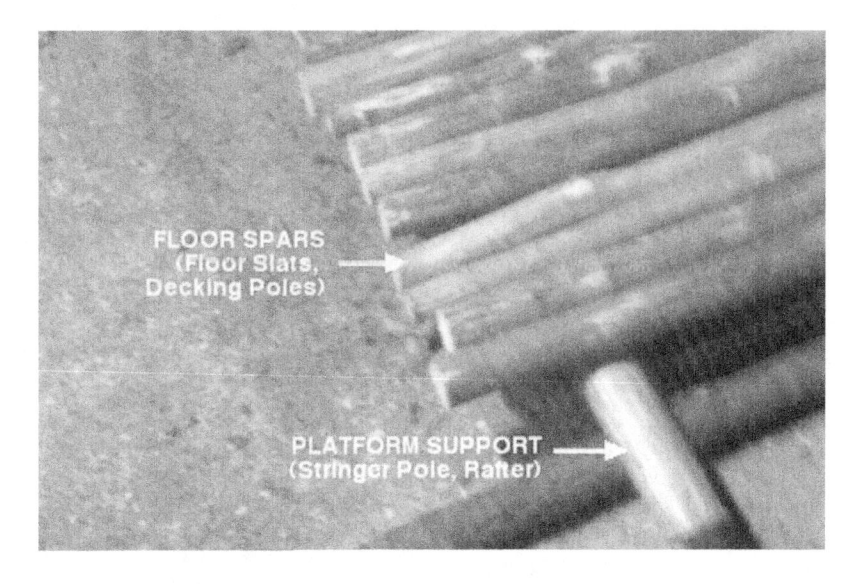

FLOOR SPARS
(Floor Slats, Decking Poles)

PLATFORM SUPPORT
(Stringer Pole, Rafter)

In the past, illustrating this lashing via written instructions, even with accurate photos, has always been a challenge. Of course, it's much better to observe the lashing actually being tied. The how-to video goes a long way to bring this process to life.

Start by tying a Clove Hitch around the platform support. Next, make a bight in the running end and pass it over the first floor pole on the *inside* of the platform support. Now, grab this bight from below and pass it underneath the platform support, and loop it over the first floor pole on the outside of the platform support.

SKILLS: Floor Lashing

Tighten both loops around the first floor pole by pulling the running end, which is extending out from the top of the platform floor between the first and second floor poles. Form another bight in the running end and repeat the same process for each subsequent floor pole until you reach the other end.

When you reach the other end, tie off the rope to the platform support with two or more, tight half hitches.

SCOUT PIONEERING — Ol' Fashioned Outdoor Fun!

View "How to Tie a Double Floor Lashing" http://www.programresources.org/floor-lashing/

- Butterfly Knot & Rope Tackle -

The **Butterfly Knot** is definitely a favorite. It's easy to tie, doesn't cause undo stress to the rope's fibers, and can be untied with relative ease, even after a heavy strain—just pull on the "wings." *Because of these advantages, the Butterfly Knot is often thought to be the preferred knot for use in a rope tackle.*

The "King of Knots" is the Bowline. It forms a fixed loop at the end of a line. The Butterfly Knot has been referred to as the "Queen of Knots," and forms a fixed loop somewhere along the middle of a line.

> *"The Butterfly Knot is without question the best knot for making a nonslip loop in the bight of a rope, and is so easy to make, one can only wonder why it is not in more general use." — John Sweet*

SCOUT PIONEERING — Ol' Fashioned Outdoor Fun!

Here's how Adolph lays out the process:

1. Start with an overhand loop, then twist the rope to form a second overhand loop. Next drop the upper loop down in back.
2. When the upper loop is dropped down, pull it under the two crossed standing parts of the rope. Then pull it up through the top loops to complete the knot.
3. To pull the knot tight, pull the upper loop while holding the standing parts of the rope at the bottom.

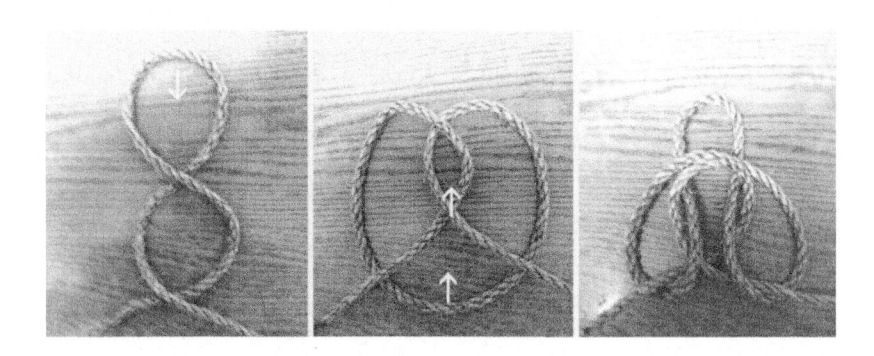

View "How to Tie a Butterfly Knot" http://www.programresources.org/butterfly-knot/

SKILLS: Butterfly Knot & Rope Tackle

A Scout puts healthy strain on a line by pulling on the hauling end of a rope tackle.

Simply put, a **rope tackle** is the way to go when you want to pull more than your own strength will permit. The idea is similar to that of a tackle using blocks and pulleys. Because once it's configured and tied off, the line is secure and tension is easily adjusted, the rope tackle can be considered an essential Scout Pioneering skill.

In a rope tackle, one end of the rope has to be anchored around a spar or tied through a ring or other piece of hardware that doesn't move. Then a knot is tied along the standing part of the rope forming a fixed loop. This loop acts as the wheel in a block. For good reasons, the Butterfly Knot is often the knot of choice for this job.

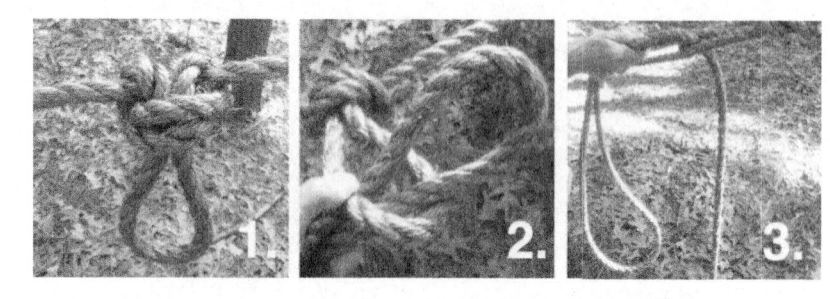

1. Start with a Butterfly Knot in the desired position along the standing part of the rope.

2. Feed the running end through the Butterfly Knot's fixed loop. When there's lots of line, make a bight in the running end and feed *it* through the fixed loop.

3. To tighten the line, grab a hold of the bight and pull it towards the anchor.

SKILLS: Butterfly Knot & Rope Tackle

4. When the desired tension is put on the line, with one hand, keep the line taut, and holding the bight in the other hand, use the bight to form a half hitch around both tight lines.

5. As the half hitch is secured, maintain the tension on the line by pinching the standing part, making sure it doesn't slip.

6. Still maintaining the tension on the tightened lines in the standing part, cinch the half hitch up close to the fixed loop of the Butterfly Knot and apply a second half hitch.

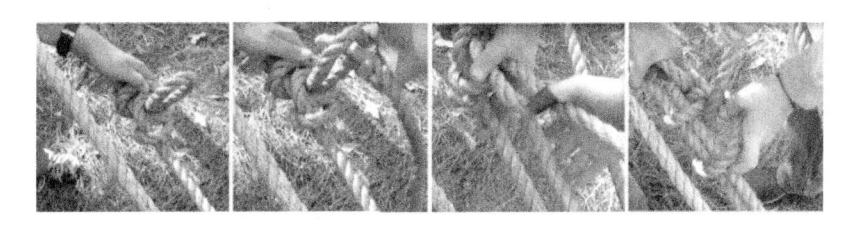

Tying a Rope Tackle to the Foot Rope of a Monkey Bridge

The rope tackle has many uses.

- It's the go-to approach for varying the strain on guylines to stabilize a structure that isn't freestanding.
- It's an effective way to adjust the tension on the foot and hand ropes of a monkey bridge.
- Known as a trucker's hitch, it's what is used to tie down and secure equipment on a trailer or truck.
- It's very useful for tightening guy lines on large tents and flies.

For safety reasons, a Taut-Line Hitch should never be relied upon to withstand heavy strain on a line. Its function is to adjust the tension on a line and will sometimes slide even when it's not supposed to.

View "How to Tie a Rope Tackle" http://www.programresources.org/rope-tackle/

SKILLS

- Roundturn with Two Half Hitches -

For pioneering and also around camp, Two Half Hitches with the addition of a simple roundturn has a variety of uses. It's known simply as a Roundturn with Two Half Hitches. In his forthright style, Adolph has given us a clear explanation. He describes how the Roundturn with Two Half Hitches is a basic knot that is very reliable for a number of uses in pioneering work. It's easy to tie and untie and doesn't reduce the strength of the rope due to sharp turns when under a hard pull.

Start off by making a roundturn. This provides extra surface around the object when chafing or slipping might be a problem. Once you've made the roundturn, the rope has a grip on whatever it's around. The strain on the rope can then be adjusted before finishing off with Two Half Hitches.

SCOUT PIONEERING — Ol' Fashioned Outdoor Fun!

This configuration is well suited for both ends of a guyline. When it's used in a place where you don't have easy access, as at the top of a tower, secure the running end, (after the Two Half Hitches are tied) with a piece of light cord.

A Guyline Attached to a Vertical Spar with an Extra Roundturn for Additional Grip

View "How to Tie a Roundturn with Two Half Hitches" http://www.programresources.org/roundturn-with-two-half-hitches/

SKILLS

- Versatile Draw Hitch -

The Draw Hitch is a neat, quick-release knot that can hold a considerable strain. The Draw Hitch is also known as the Highwayman's Hitch. Though there is no verifiable evidence that it was ever used by robbers on horseback to unhitch their horses for a quick getaway, it is ideal for reliably securing a boat to a mooring (or horse to a hitching post) with the assurance that you can easily release the knot with a simple tug and quickly be on your way, and all you need is one hand to do it.

In addition to securing the end of a line to a fixed point, the Draw Hitch can be tied in the middle of the line resulting in two ends of the rope hanging down equally. This way, a climber can lower himself down using one end (standing part), and have the ability to retrieve the rope by tugging on the other end (free end).

In pioneering, the Draw Hitch's main function comes into play when hoisting a large structure that is not intended for climbing, e.g. a tall gateway, and the lines you're using for lifting and preventing over-pulling are not guylines. Tie the middle of the hoisting ropes to the structure with Draw Hitches. Then, when the structure is standing, these lines can be easily removed with a simple tug on the free end.

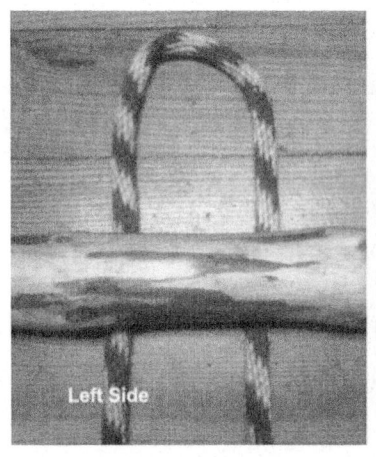

Place a large bight in the desired part of the line, behind the spar. Form a small bight on the left side, under the spar, and carry it over the front.

SKILLS: *Draw Hitch*

Pass this left side bight through the top of the large bight. Tighten this by pulling up on the left side bight and down on the right side.

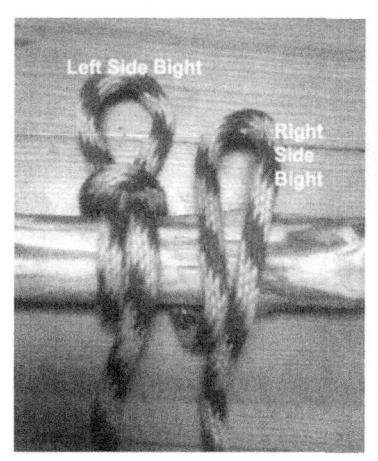

Now, form a small bight on the right side, under the spar, and carry it over the front. Pass this right side bight through the left side bight.

SCOUT PIONEERING — Ol' Fashioned Outdoor Fun!

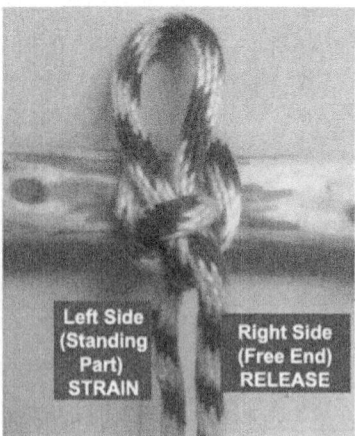

Apply strain by pulling on the left. Release the knot by pulling on the right.

Great for binding coils of rope!

"The Draw Hitch is definitely a fun knot—fun to make and use." — *John Sweet*

View "How to Tie a Draw Hitch" http://www.programresources.org/draw-hitch/

SKILLS

- Essential Rolling Hitch -

John Thurman lists the Rolling Hitch (also known as a Magnus Hitch) as one of the essential pioneering knots. It's similar to a Clove Hitch, but is a lot less likely to slip under a sideways pull. When securing a guyline to a vertical spar, the Rolling Hitch can be used in lieu of a Roundturn with Two Half Hitches. It's also useful to attach a rope to another rope that has strain on it. Make sure that the direction of the pull exerted on the Rolling Hitch is against the double strand.

It's interesting to know that the basic knot: two half-hitches, also known as a Double Half Hitch, is in actuality a Clove Hitch tied around the standing part of a line. After all, in the BSA, the knot *is* referred to as: "Two Half Hitches," and of course, that's exactly what a Clove Hitch *is*—two half hitches! So, it should come as no surprise, especially with the way it's

SCOUT PIONEERING — Ol' Fashioned Outdoor Fun!

used to reduce the tendency for a hitch to slide in the direction of a pull, that another basic and oft-used knot, the Taut-Line Hitch, is in actuality a *Rolling Hitch* tied around the standing part of a line.

When the Rolling Hitch is tied to a spar, pull can be exerted either perpendicular to or along the length of the spar. When you need extra gripping power, just add extra turns.

Start by laying the running end over the pole. Next, make a roundturn around the pole.

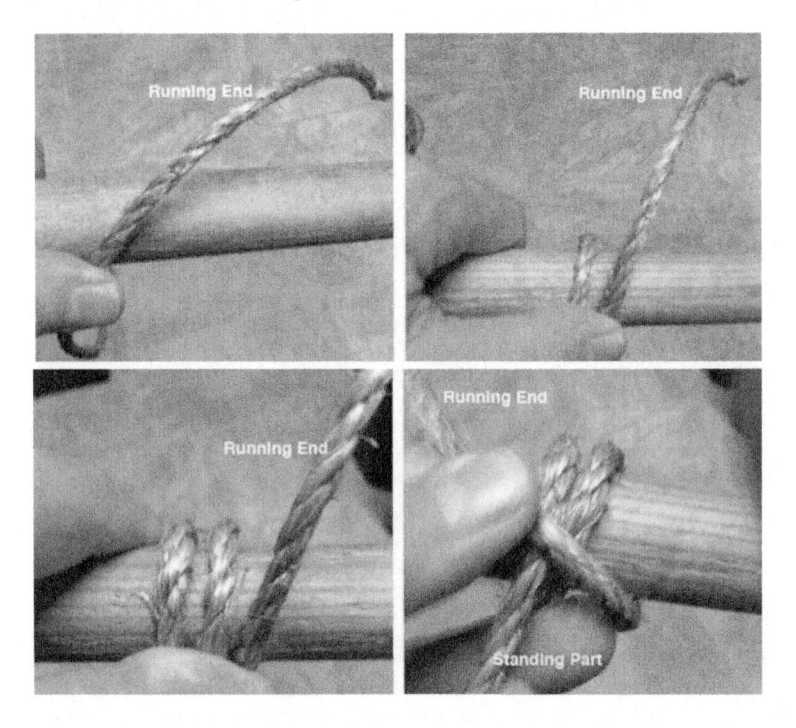

SKILLS: Rolling Hitch

Complete the roundturn and hold the running end up. Now cross the running end over the standing part.

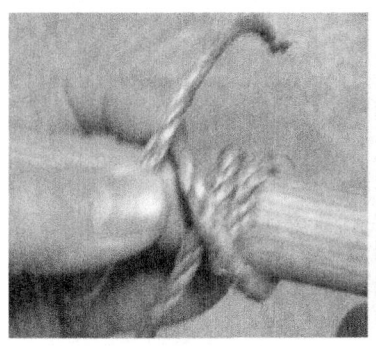

Make another turn around the pole on the other side of the roundturn, and then form a half hitch by tucking the running end under the turn. Pull it tight.

When you want to attach a light tackle or ring to a vertical pole, reeve a short line through the tackle or ring, double the rope over to form a bight, and tie a Rolling Hitch with the bight, around the fixed object.

To form a hand or shoulder loop to carry a spar, tie two Rolling Hitches, one at each end of a short rope.

Two Rolling Hitches Forming a Handle.

View "How to Tie a Rolling Hitch" http://www.programresources.org/rolling-hitch/

SKILLS

- Dual-Purpose Scaffold Hitch -

Primary Role: This is an effective knot to use when suspending the seats for a swing or for the plank on a swing boat.

Scaffold Hitches Rigged With Bowlines

When rigging Scaffold Hitches for structures with swings, it's a good idea to cut notches about 4 inches from the ends of the board to give the rope something to bite into.

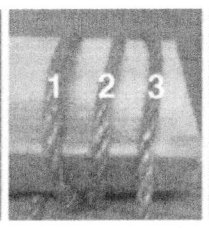

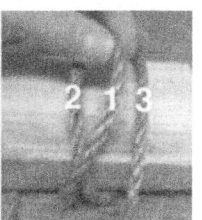

Lay the rope over one end of the board and make three wraps. Take hold of the first wrap and lay it over the second.

99

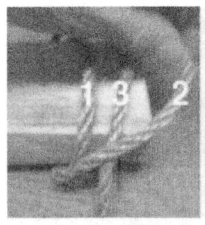

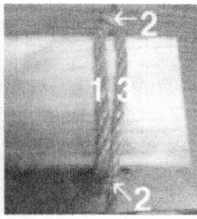

Next, take hold of the second wrap, carry to over the first and third wraps, and continue over and then under the end of the board. To form the hitch, pull both rope ends tight, and position them so the board is held in place.

Secondary Role: Many different knots can be used for tying up bundles of sticks or poles, but when it comes to bundling 3 to 4-foot ladder rungs, platform spars, and walkway cross spars, the Scaffold Hitch provides superior clinching power. This is exactly what is needed to keep the bundles tight.

With the middle of the rope, make three wraps, working your way towards the end of the bundle. Take hold of the first wrap and lay it over the second. Next, take hold of the second wrap and carry it over both the first and the third wraps and around the bundle. Pull both ends tight and

SKILLS: Scaffold Hitch

wrap the remaining length of both ends tightly around the bundle. Finish the hitch by binding the ends down with a Square Knot.

SCOUT PIONEERING — Ol' Fashioned Outdoor Fun!

- Dependable Constrictor Knot -

Also known as the Miller's Knot and Bag Knot, this is truly an effective binding knot. In the past it was relied upon to secure the tops of bags containing flour and gun powder. You'll find it has many practical camping and pioneering uses.

The constructor is based on the Clove Hitch, except after the first half hitch, the running end forms a half knot with the standing part. It's this half-knot that provides additional hold when the hitch is pulled tight.

1. Make a turn around the spar with the running end, then cross over the standing part of the rope.
2. Carry the running end under the spar.
3. Cross the running end on the outside of and over the standing part.

SKILLS: Constrictor Knot

4. Form a half knot by passing it underneath the half hitch.

When you are applying a Mark II Square Lashing to a vertical spar, and you need to provide an extra measure of gripping power to minimize the crossing spar's tendency to slip down when under a heavy strain, you can place the midpoint of the lashing rope around the pole with a Constrictor Knot.

Here's a convenient way to tie a Constrictor Knot in the standing part of the rope over an open spar:

1. Make a right overhand loop.
2. While holding the left side of the loop, twist down on the right side counter clockwise making a right underhand loop.
3. Place this second loop behind the standing part and pass it under the first loop.

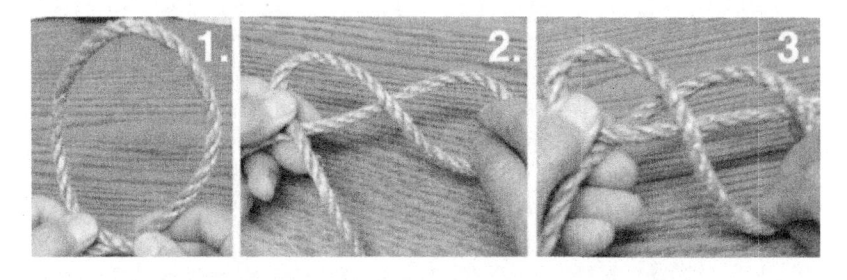

4. Grab hold of both loops and place then over the spar.
5. Pull tight.

SKILLS: Constrictor Knot

In pioneering, the Constrictor Knot can be used interchangeably with a Clove Hitch, except once the Constrictor Knot is pulled tight, it's quite hard to untie.

Two Scouts, with a combined weight of 550 lbs, test the strength of the lashings, *started with Constrictor Knots,* holding up the roller bar supports of this Camp Seesaw.

View "How to Tie a Constrictor Knot http://www.programresources.org/constrictor-knot/

- Useful Prusik -

A pulley inside the loop of a rope grommet is tied to the end of a pole with a Prusik.

Adolph puts it like this in his superb edition of the pioneering merit badge pamphlet: "The Prusik has the reputation of having a firm, sure grip once it is put under pressure. The multiple opposing turns provide friction and put a bend in the standing part of the rope, which becomes more difficult to pass through the turns as a lateral pull is applied."

The Prusik has long been used by climbers to form sliding hand and foot holds with a smaller rope around one with a larger diameter.

In pioneering, like the Rolling Hitch, the Prusik can be used to effectively attach a ring or light tackle to a spar.

SKILLS: Prusik

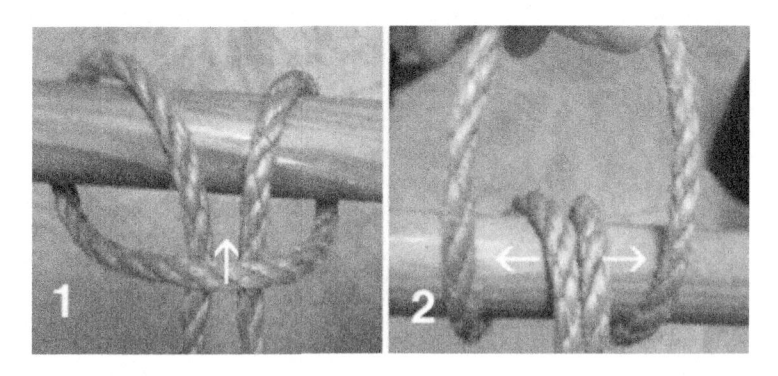

- String a ring or tackle inside the loop of a rope grommet.
- Attach the grommet to the pole with a Lark's Head.

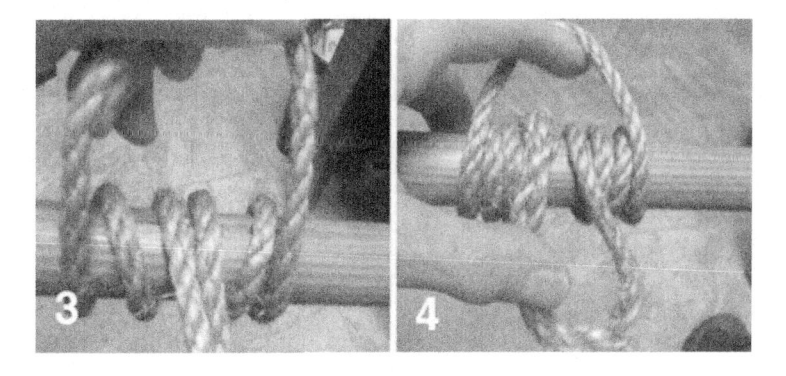

- Inside the middle of the Lark's Head, wrap the loop around the pole at least two complete times.
- When finished, position the Prusik and pull the loop tight.

View "How to Tie a Lark's Head Video http://www.programresources.org/larks-head/

- Half Knot Round Lashing -

When extending the length of two poles with larger diameters or when joining several short poles together, the Half Knot (West Country) Round Lashing is an excellent choice. This approach, consisting of a series of tight half knots and ending with a Square Knot to join two parallel poles, yields a connection that is strong and dependable. Though it takes a little more effort to untie than a common round lashing made with its series of wraps beginning and ending with a Clove Hitch, this form of round lashing remains intact better and provides more resistance to coming loose.

The Half Knot Round Lashing is formed by simply tying a series of

SKILLS: Half Knot Round Lashing

identical, interlocking half-knots around both poles. Tie one half-knot in front and the next half-knot in back. Make sure each half-knot is tied flush against the one that precedes it and pulled up as tightly as possible.

After tying six to ten half-knots, finish off the lashing with a Square Knot. When the structure needs to resist more strain or last for a longer period, tying a tight Half Knot Round Lashing near both ends where the two poles intersect is the obvious choice to maintain a rigid connection.

A half knot is often called an overhand knot. The distinction is, an overhand knot is tied at the end of a line, often used as a stopper knot, and the half knot is tied around an object.

SCOUT PIONEERING — Ol' Fashioned Outdoor Fun!

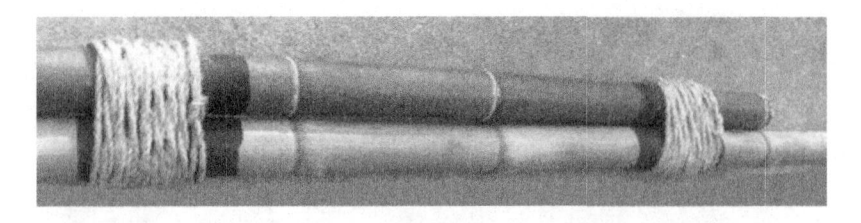

Two Half Knot Round Lashings join long lengths of bamboo for a tall flagpole.

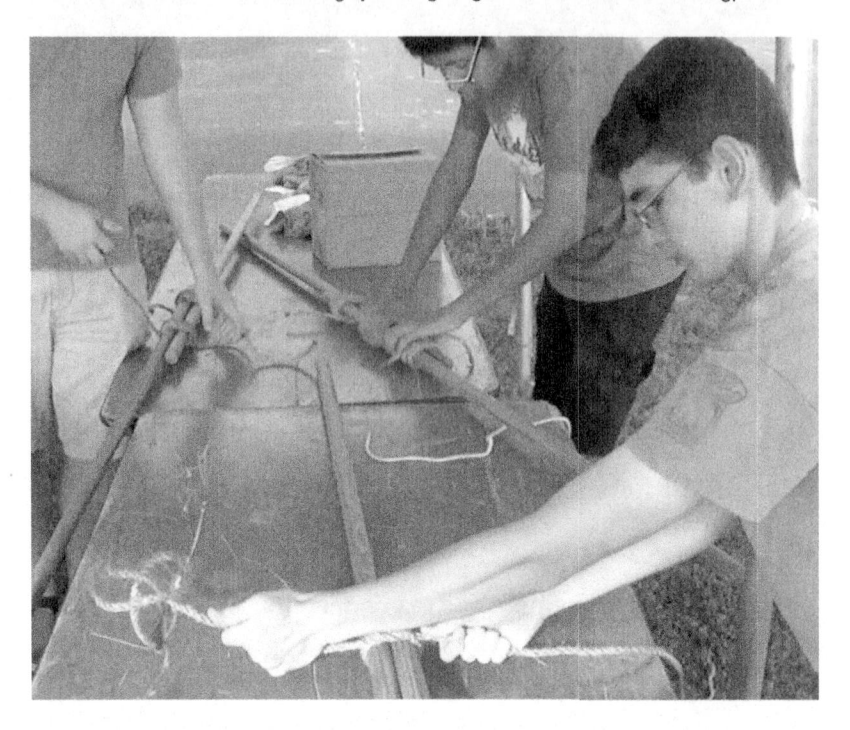

Scouts rely upon ten Half Knot Round Lashings to join six poles together to build a 24 foot Scout Stave flagpole.

View "How to Tie a Half Knot (West Country) Round Lashing"
http://www.programresources.org/west-country-round-lashing/

SKILLS

- Whipping Lashing Ropes -

Half Knot (West Country) Whipping – Formed in the same way as the Half Knot Round Lashing, this is the method the pioneering staff is directed to use to whip the ends of the hundreds of lashing ropes for building the structures in the pioneering area at the national jamboree. Using this approach to whip rope is easier to learn and easier to tie. The bottom line is, it holds much better than most other methods.

1. Start with a tight, half knot.
2. Apply an identical half knot on the opposite side.
3. Repeat the process until the whipping is as wide as the rope's diameter, and finish with a Square Knot.

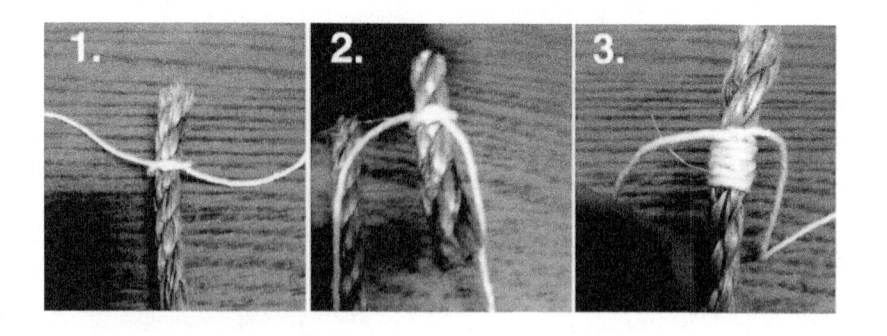

View "How to Tie a Half Knot (West Country) Whipping"
http://www.programresources.org/half-knot-west-country-whipping/

Sailmaker's Whipping – The sheets of sails flailing around in the wind required a type of whipping that could withstand continual stress. The Sailmaker's Whipping provided the solution, and is still the best way to whip a lashing rope to avoid the ends unravelling. It takes a little more practice to master, but it's a worthwhile whipping method to embrace. It's also really cool.

SKILLS: Whipping Lashing Ropes

My first exposure to this form of whipping occurred when I was a new Cub Scout in the late 50's.

Get ready to begin.

Unlay the three strands about an inch or so.

Feel free to mark strand 1.

Spread out the strands for easy access.

113

SCOUT PIONEERING — Ol' Fashioned Outdoor Fun!

My older brother's friend, an avid Boy Scout, demonstrated the process.

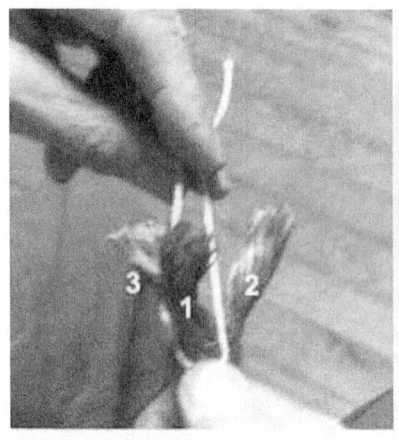

Make a bight in the whipping cord and slip the loop over strand 1, between strands 2 & 3.

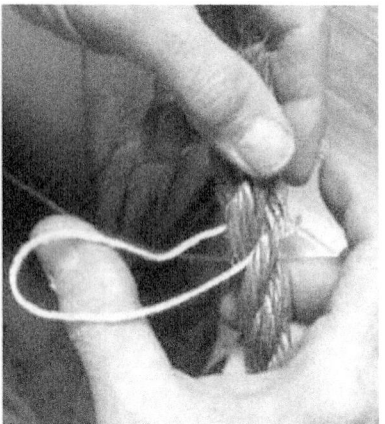

Relay the three strands.

Holding the bight and the rope in one hand, take the long end of the cord in the other hand.

SKILLS: Whipping Lashing Ropes

He remained silent the whole time—didn't say a word as he methodically worked with the rope and the whipping cord.

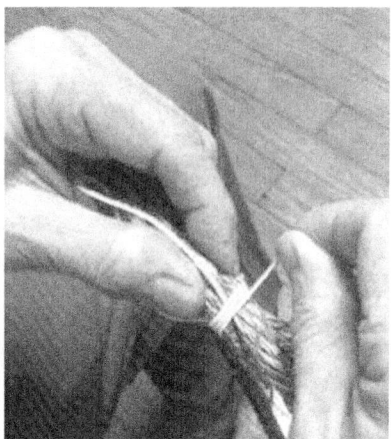

Begin to wrap the long end of whipping cord around the rope.

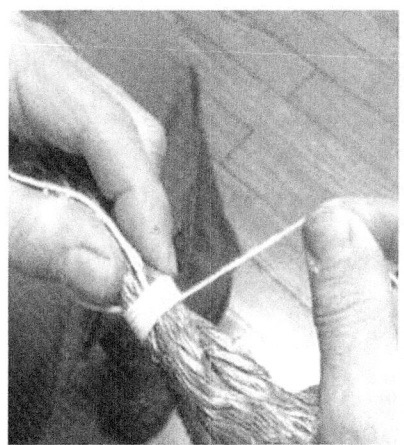

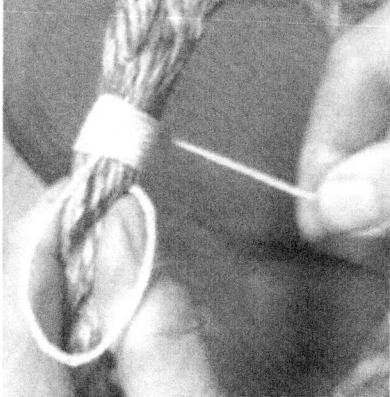

Continue wrapping tightly.

SCOUT PIONEERING — Ol' Fashioned Outdoor Fun!

He slowly and carefully completed each step, as I stood by watching his hands.

Done wrapping.

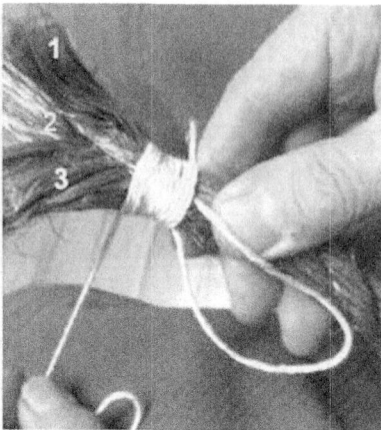

Unlay the three strands

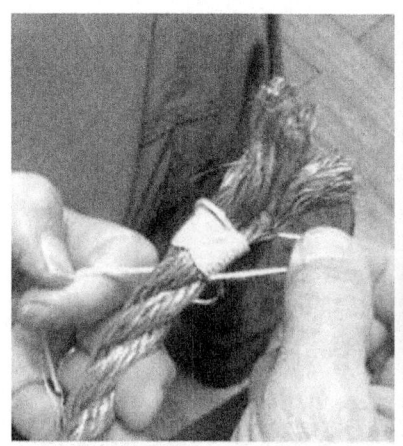

Take hold of the loop and slip it over strand 1.

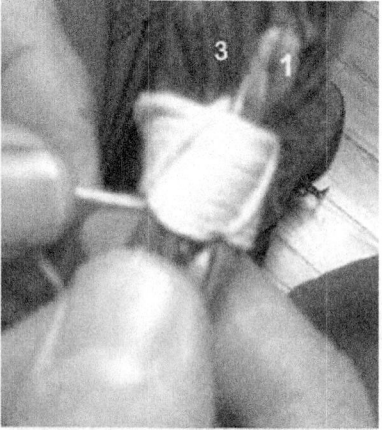

With the short end of the whipping cord, pull the loop tight over strand 1.

SKILLS: Whipping Lashing Ropes

When he was done, with pride in his voice, he held up the completed whipping and smilingly declared ...

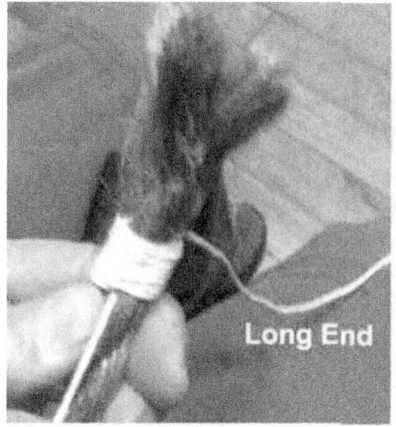

Place the long end of the whipping cord between strands 1 & 3.

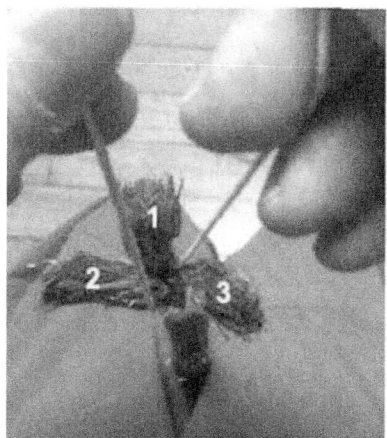

Place the short end of the whipping cord between strands 2 & 3.

Join the short and long ends of the whipping cord with a square (reef) knot.

SCOUT PIONEERING — Ol' Fashioned Outdoor Fun!

"And that's how you whip a rope."

Pull it tight.

Twist the top strands of the rope back together.

Trim the excess off the top.

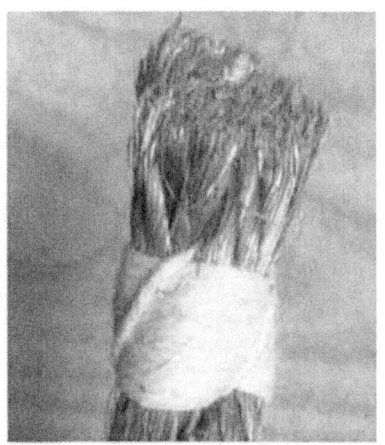

View "How to Tie a Sailmaker's Whipping" http://www.programresources.org/sailmakers-whipping/

SKILLS

- Optional Diagonal Lashing -

This lashing can be used when there is a need to close a gap between two poles where they cross each other but do not touch. (The Mark II Square Lashing can readily serve the same purpose, because applying strain when completing the first wrap will effectively draw the poles together like the Timber Hitch does in beginning a traditional diagonal lashing, or like the Lark's Head does when tying the Filipino version. The advantage of applying a square lashing is that more rope actually comes in contact with the surface area of the poles.)

It's still appropriate to point out, the diagonal lashing gets its name from the fact the wraps are formed diagonally to the poles. It has nothing to do with the poles crossing one another at less than 90°.

SCOUT PIONEERING — Ol' Fashioned Outdoor Fun!

1. Cinch the poles together by tying a timber hitch around them where they cross.
2. Make three to four wrapping turns on the opposite diagonal to the Timber Hitch. Keep the wraps parallel to one another and pull them tight.
3. Make three more tight wraps across the first three, again keeping them parallel.

SKILLS: *Diagonal Lashing*

4. Take two to three frapping turns between the poles, tightly around both sets of wraps and complete the lashing with a Clove Hitch around one of the poles.

As with these X-braces, the center lashing serves to spring the spars together, closing the gap between them where they cross, forming triangles, resisting racking, and providing stability.

View "How to Tie a Diagonal Lashing" http://www.programresources.org/diagonal-lashing/

CHAPTER 5

ACTIVITIES

Merely teaching a knot or lashing and then holding practice sessions is going to get boring very quickly. So, as soon as Scouts are enabled to put a skill into action, have them do just that! *Activity-based instruction* includes a welcome opportunity for Scouts to get involved using the skill—in a fun way. *Using* the skill, even with something as mundane as a race, brings the skill to life. But, the best kinds of activities are not only fun while serving to reinforce the Scout's ability; they actually illustrate what the skill can accomplish!

There are a host of Scout skill challenges that call to action a wide range of basic pioneering skills. Many are illustrated with videos of real Scouts actively engaged during their troop meeting. During these activities, Scouts are focused and involved. They're also having a blast!

When the required materials call for poles larger than Scout staves, generally speaking the size of the spars listed in the materials are *the same size* required to build the Double A-Frame Monkey Bridge and many other projects. This is very convenient, because besides being great projects to start with, these basic pioneering structures are popular favorites! Also, there are obvious advantages to having the same materials that will be needed to build structures out in the field, available during these troop meeting challenges.

Building pioneering projects is replete with numerous positive outcomes. So are these troop meeting, Scout skill, challenge activities. In addition to using the skills and having fun, Scouts also get to use teamwork, cooperate with one another, overcome obstacles, experience success, and show Scout spirit!

ACTIVITIES

- Vertical Hitching Race -

Applying Hitches over an Open-ended Pole

<u>Half Hitches on an Open Pole</u> – Along with a variety of useful applications around the campsite, this skill is essential when attaching the hand ropes to the A-frames of a monkey bridge. Once Scouts get the knack, this activity is really fun.

Materials: 15-foot braided nylon or polyester cords attached at the bottom of one or more 4-foot upright poles

Method: Scouts apply a succession of over-an-end half hitches (underhand loops) over the upright pole(s).

Scoring: The Scout who applies the most half hitches in a set amount of seconds is the winner.

Scouts race to see who can place half hitches over a vertical pole most quickly.

View "Troop Meeting Challenge: Hitching Race" http://www.programresources.org/hitching-challenge-video/

ACTIVITIES

- Horizontal Hitching Race -

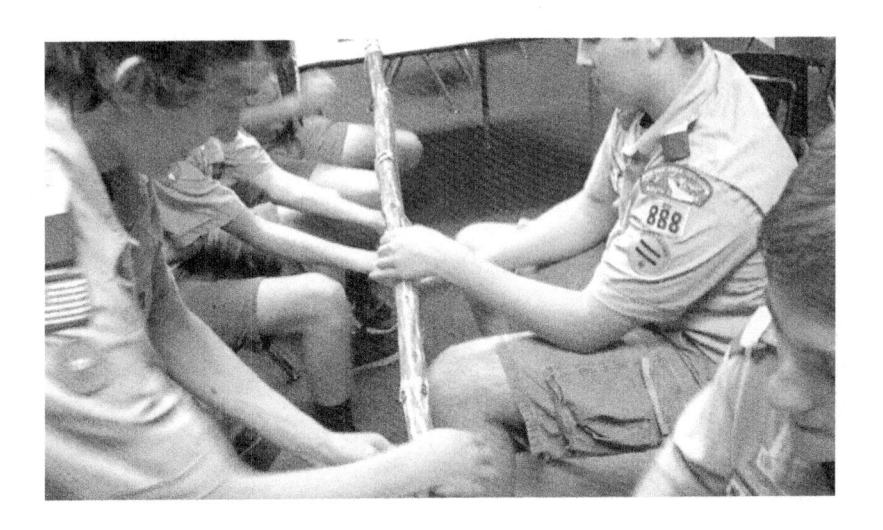

Half Hitches on a Closed Pole – This skill makes it easy to effectively snug a Clove Hitch tight up against the wraps, when finishing a tripod, shear, round, "clove-hitch-square lashing," or diagonal lashing.

Materials: horizontal pole(s) set up waist-high with pairs of 3-foot lengths of pliable cord, attached and hanging down. Each Scout should have two cords right next to each other, set apart from other pairs of cords leaving enough space to apply the half hitches without interfering with the Scout(s) next to him.

Method: On signal, Scouts race to tie a series of four half hitches with each cord, one cord proceeding from the left, and the other proceeding from the right. When they have completed all eight half hitches, they yell out, "done!"

Variation: Tie the two pairs of cords about a foot from the ends of a Scout stave. Scouts pair up and sitting down either next to or across from one another, they race to tie the half hitches with the stave balanced on their laps.

Scoring: The first Scout to correctly complete all eight half hitches around their section of the pole wins that round.

View "Patrol Challenge: Horizontal Half Hitching Race" http://www.programresources.org/horizontal-half-hitching-race-video/

ACTIVITIES

- Joining Staves -

Raising Them Up!

Round Lashing – This is a fun way to put a newly-acquired round lashing skill into action. It's involving, challenging, and demonstrates how the technique is applied.

Materials: plenty of 6-foot lashing ropes and a large supply of Scout staves

Method: In the time allotted, Scouts join as many Scout staves together with two round lashings as they can, into one long connected pole. When they are done, they lift the entire joined-together construction over their heads.

Scoring: The longest, intact collection of staves wins.

Variation: If presented out of doors, Scouts can try to hold their long, joined poles vertically!

Scoring: The patrol who can hold up the longest collection of staves wins.

Scouts give out a yell as they hold up their collection of joined-together staves.

View "Troop Meeting Activity: Joining Staves" http://www.programresources.org/joining-staves-video/

ACTIVITIES

- Catch the Snapper -

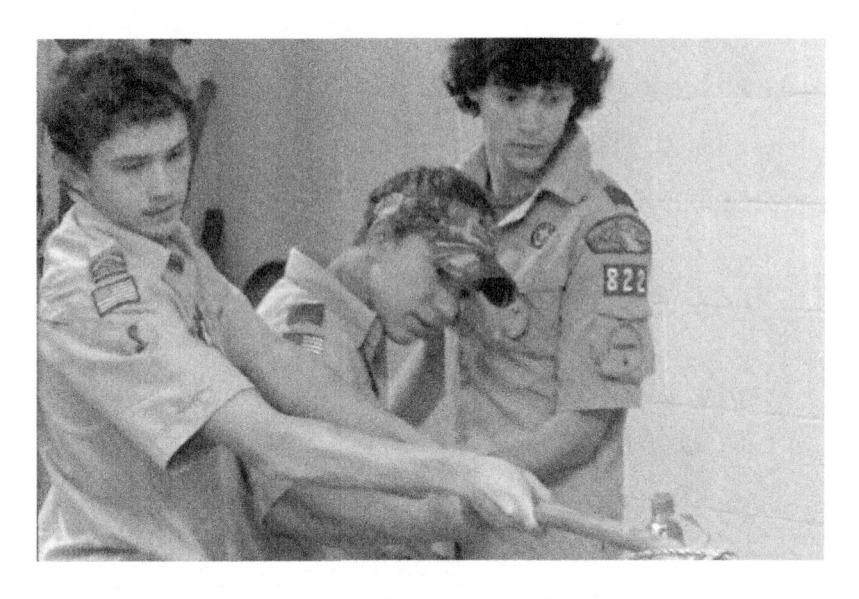

Concentration and Cooperation

<u>Round Lashing</u> – Always a favorite, this activity is a race that requires some quick thinking and lots of cooperation.

Materials: four Scout staves, six 6-foot lashing ropes, one 3-foot cord, one fishing sinker and one or more mouse or rattraps for each patrol

Method: Form a "river" by marking two parallel lines 15 feet apart. The patrols line up on one "riverbank." 15 feet away is a cocked mouse or rattrap. Patrols build a long fishing pole by joining the staves with round lashings and attaching the sinker to the end which is then used to catch the "snapper(s)." The patrol must use all the issued materials.

Scoring: The first patrol to lift the mouse or rattrap up by catching it on their fishing sinker wins.

A Triumphant Moment!

View Patrol Challenge: Catch the Snapper http://www.programresources.org/catch-the-snapper-video/

ACTIVITIES

- Scout Stave Flagpole Race -

Putting Teamwork and Skills into Action!

<u>Round Lashing, Roundturn with Two Half Hitches or Rolling Hitch, Taut-Line Hitch, Strop Lashing</u> – This is an activity that leads to a patrol's increased ability to impressively erect a flagpole in the field.

Materials: for each patrol, four Scout staves (or three Scout staves if their patrol flag is already secured to a pole), six 6-foot lashing ropes, three 15-foot cords, three stakes, one mallet, small flag with grommets, two short cords to attach the flag to the flagpole

Method: On signal, each patrol flies their flag on their flagpole by: joining the staves together with round lashings, tying on their flag with strop lashings (page 239), attaching the three guylines about 3/4 of the way up from the bottom with Round Turns with Two Half Hitches (or Rolling Hitches), hammering in the three stakes forming an equilateral triangle, tying the guylines at the stakes with Taut-Line Hitches, and adjusting the tension on the lines to securely hold their flagpole in a tight, vertical position.

Scoring: Patrols can receive points for both speed and efficiency.

View "Patrol Challenge: Raising a Flagpole Demonstration"
http://www.programresources.org/flagpole-race-demo-video/

ACTIVITIES

- A-Frame Chariot Race -

A-Frame Chariot Race Orchestrated Indoors

<u>Square Lashing, Shear Lashing</u> – Any activity that's a race where you get to ride something, has got to be fun. What's more, building A-frames is as fundamental as you can get. Provide the same materials Scouts will use for the projects they'll be building.

Materials: two 8-foot x 4-inch spars, one 6-foot x 3-inch spar, three 15-20-foot x 1/4-inch manila lashing ropes for each patrol

SCOUT PIONEERING — Ol' Fashioned Outdoor Fun!

Method: On signal, patrols lash together an A-frame using a shear lashing at the tips of the 8-foot spars and square lashings at the butt ends for the 6-foot ledger. (If they choose, Scouts can elect to tie three square lashings.) When the A-frame is built, it is either dragged or carried around a pre-set course or to a turn-around-line and back. The course is to be completed in accordance with whatever guidelines are established beforehand.

Scoring: The fastest patrol to complete the race wins.

Note: Dragging the A-frame can cause damage to indoor floors, carpeting, and outdoor grassy areas, and should only be done on durable surfaces.

View "Patrol Challenge: A-Frame Chariot Race" http://www.programresources.org/a-frame-chariot-race-video/

ACTIVITIES

- Crossing the Alligator Pit -

Well-Coordinated Teamwork!

<u>Square Lashing, Shear Lashing</u> – Building and rigging this A-frame walker is one thing; keeping the rider aloft and helping him move across the "pit" is quite another. This is a super, team building opportunity!

Materials: for each patrol, two 8-foot x 4-inch spars, one sturdy 6-foot x 3-inch spar, three 15-foot lashing ropes, six 20-

foot guylines 1/4-inch in diameter, a minimum of seven participating patrol members

Method: Mark the "alligator pit" on the ground; it should be 15 feet across and as wide as necessary to accommodate all the patrols. The patrols line up on one side of the pit. On signal, they lash together an A-frame "walker," using a shear lashing at the top and square lashings at the cross bar, or three square lashings. Near the top, with Two Half Hitches, they attach two guylines, and at each bottom corner they attach two more. The patrol then stands the walker upright and one member climbs on the crossbar. Scouts control each guyline and "walk" the A-frame across the pit by tipping it from side to side and moving it forward.

Scoring: The first patrol to finish wins. This, like other activities, can be a timed contest if there aren't enough materials for all patrols. *Note:* Crossing the Alligator Pit indoors can cause damage to floors and carpeting, and should only be done on durable surfaces.

View "Patrol Challenge: Crossing the Alligator Pit"
http://www.programresources.org/crossing-the-alligator-pit-video/

ACTIVITIES

- Ladder Building -

Relying on the Lashings AND on their Patrol!

<u>Square Lashing</u> – Building something for climbing is always a hit! This pioneering Scout skill challenge not only provides patrol members with a golden opportunity to trust the soundness of their lashings, but also to really trust their patrol mates who are depended upon to safely hold up the square-lashed construction.

Materials: for each patrol: two 8-foot x 4-inch spars, four 3 to 4-foot x 2-inch ladder rungs, eight 15-foot lashing ropes

Method: Each patrol will lash together a ladder with four rungs, spacing them *from the bottom, about 1-foot apart,* using eight square lashings. When sturdy, the whole patrol will stand the ladder up. While one patrol member at a time takes a turn climbing to the top rung, the rest of the entire patrol *attentively* holds their ladder steady with both hands.

View "Patrol Challenge: Ladder Building Activity" http://www.programresources.org/ladder-building-video/

ACTIVITIES

- Everyone on the Tripod -

All Aboard!

<u>Tripod Lashing, Square Lashing</u> – Definitely an all-time favorite, along with honing their lashing prowess and ability to work as a team, this activity can enhance patrol spirit like none other.

SCOUT PIONEERING — Ol' Fashioned Outdoor Fun!

Materials: for each patrol, three 8-foot x 4-inch spars, three sturdy 6-foot x 3-inch spars, six 15-foot lashing ropes, one 20-foot lashing rope.

Method: On signal, each patrol builds a tripod with the 8-foot spars, and the 20-foot rope. When finished, they lash a 6-foot spar between each of the legs. When the tripod is strong and secure, all the patrol members stand on the 6-foot spars, making sure their weight is evenly distributed.

Scoring: First patrol with all its members off the ground wins.

View "Patrol Challenge: Everyone on the Tripod" http://www.programresources.org/everyone-on-the-tripod-video/

View "Everyone on the Tripod (Demonstration)" http://www.programresources.org/everyone-on-the-tripod-video-demonstration/

ACTIVITIES

- Reactor Transporter -

Concentration and Control

<u>Tripod Lashing, Square Lashing</u> – Connecting an equilateral triangle to a tripod yields a neat gadget comprised of four triangles. Carefully carrying the structure with precision is another matter. Slow and steady wins the race!

Materials: for each patrol, six Scout staves, six 6-foot lashing ropes, one 10-foot lashing rope, two 3-foot light cords, one No. 10 can with a bail attached, and a large washer or nut from a 1/2-inch bolt

Method: On signal, each patrol builds a transporter by lashing a three-sided frame with three staves, and then lashing on a tripod from the three corners of the frame. The can is suspended from the top of the tripod. The washer or nut is also hung from the top of the tripod. It hangs down into the can, but does not touch the bottom or the sides. When finished, three patrol members pick the transporter up by its three corners and carry it to a turn-around point and back. If the suspended washer or nut swings and hits the side of the can, the patrol must return to the starting line and start the carry again. The object is to transport the reactor so gently and evenly that it is not jarred.

Scoring: The fastest time wins.

View: "Patrol Challenge: Reactor Transporter" http://www.programresources.org/reactor-transporter-video/

ACTIVITIES

- Lift Seat Procession -

A Parade of "Privileged Characters"

<u>Floor Lashing</u> – Learning a useful lashing and then putting it into action to carry their patrol mate is a joyous way to bring the skill to life. In addition to experiencing a practical application for the floor lashing, when this mobile carrying platform is soundly constructed, and the Scout is seated with appropriate confidence, this patrol mate can rightfully feel

special—the grand center of attention. This activity is not a race. It's more like a parade.

Materials: two 15-foot lashing ropes, two 6-foot x 3-inch spars, four to six 3 to 4-foot x 2-inch floor spars

Method: Scouts will construct a lift seat by lashing the floor spars to the 6-foot platform supports, using two floor lashings. When completed, four Scouts carry one Scout, seated and holding on, around a predetermined course. The process is repeated a designated amount of times, carrying a different Scout each time.

Scoring: Points can be awarded in accordance with how well the platform is constructed, and how efficiently the patrols use their lift seats to carry their members.

View "Patrol Challenge: Lift Seat Procession" http://www.programresources.org/lift-seat-challenge-video/

ACTIVITIES

- Roman Chariot Race -

Illustration by John Sweet

<u>Trestle Building</u> – This activity originated at Gilwell in the early days of Leader Training and for many years was used on every Scout Wood Badge Course as a classic demonstration of Baden-Powell's patrol method in action:

- the patrol as the unit of activity
- the immediate application of newly acquired skills

- the construction of a basic unit in mainline pioneering
- light-hearted competition between patrols

Materials: two 8-foot x 3-inch spars, two 6-foot x 2 to 3-inch spars, two 4-foot x 2 to 2-1/2-inch spars (or two more 6-foot spars), nine 15-foot lashing ropes, three 10-foot ropes per patrol

Method: Each patrol lashes together a trestle, using the 8-foot spars as the legs, the 6-foot spars as the cross braces, and the 4-foot spars as the ledgers. The chariot is dragged to a turning line and back again, with one patrol member on board. To imitate an actual chariot to the fullest extent, two Scouts act as "wheels" keeping the chariot upright, patrol members pull the chariot like horses using two hauling lines tied to the top ledger at each leg, and the rider grabs hold of a rope with each end tied to the top of a leg, serving as the "reins"

Scoring: The first patrol all seated with their chariot taken apart and ropes coiled, after dragging their rider back to the finish line, wins. Further information: https://wp.me/p30vwr-13x

ACTIVITIES

- Rope Tackle Tug-of-War -

Two Against One (and it's no contest)

Butterfly Knot, Rope Tackle – After a skill is learned, do something with it! In an engaging and entertaining way, this routine illustrates the mechanical advantage gained by using a rope tackle.

Materials: an anchor point, one 1/2-inch diameter length of manila rope at least 20 feet long, a rope grommet rigged with a metal ring or a strop with a thimble and ring secured to the anchor point

Method: a Butterfly Knot is rigged about 10 feet from the end of the rope. That end is reeved through the anchor's ring and then passed through the fixed loop of the Butterfly Knot creating a rope tackle. Three Scouts of approximately the same weight are selected. One stands with their back to the anchor point and grabs hold of the end of the rope (hauling end) passing through the loop of the Butterfly Knot. The other two grab a hold of the other end of the rope. On signal, the single Scout pulls on the hauling end, and the other two on their end. Scouts can rotate as desired.

Variation: 1) Pit one smaller Scout at the hauling end against one larger Scout. 2) After tugging the other Scout(s), and holding them in place, the Scout on the hauling end properly ties off the rope tackle with a couple of half hitches.

View "Hands-on Demonstration: Rope Tackle Tug of War"
http://www.programresources.org/rope-tackle-tug-of-war-video/

ACTIVITIES

- Scout Stave Launcher -

Uniquely Fun!

<u>Square Lashing, Shear Lashing</u> – Who doesn't enjoy firing projectiles at a target or to see how far they can go?

Materials: six Scout staves, seven 6-foot x 1/4-inch lashing ropes, three short lengths of cord (to secure the shot holder to the structure), one pre-made "shot-holder" fashioned from a 12-1/2-ounce can https://wp.me/p30vwr-XA/ #shotholder, large supply of newspaper and masking or scotch

SCOUT PIONEERING — Ol' Fashioned Outdoor Fun!

tape, or a supply of aluminum foil (or a supply of tennis balls if the activity is outside), playing area large enough to spread out for each patrol, eye protection for the Scouts firing or holding the launcher, optional Scout stave launcher diagram http://www.programresources.org/wp-content/uploads/2016/08/ScoutStave.jpg

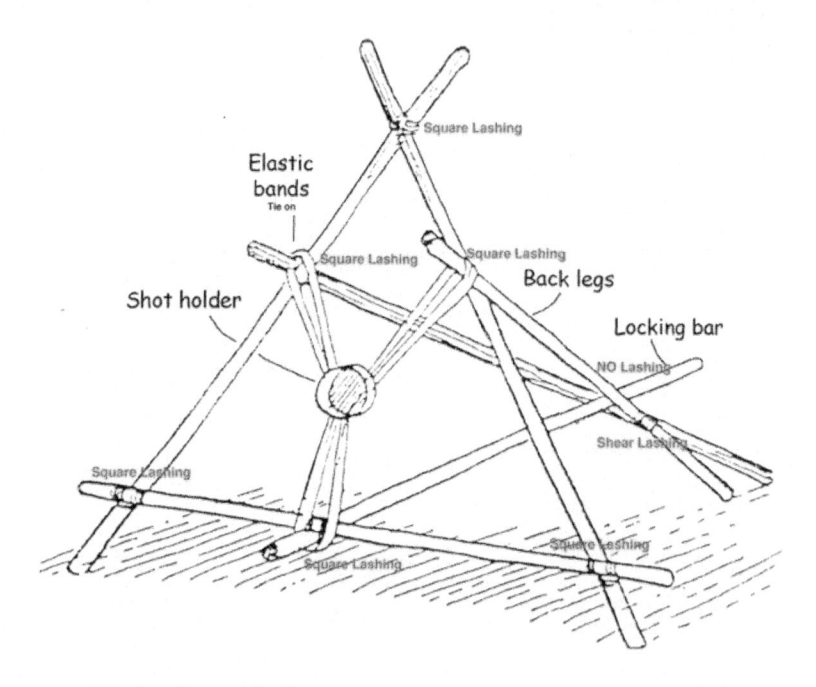

Method: An indoor or outdoor area is set up so there's plenty of room to launch the "shots." Targets can be positioned, or patrols can launch their projectiles for distance. Each patrol is provided the necessary materials along with the design

ACTIVITIES

drawing. They are each assigned their own designated area (about 10 feet x 10 feet) in which they must stay. On signal, they race to build their Scout Stave Launcher. If they're indoors, they will also have to set to work and make a supply of "shots" with the tin foil or newspaper and tape. As soon as they are ready, they can proceed to launch their "shots" at designated targets in the shooting area, or if there's enough space, they can also launch the "shots" for distance.

Scoring: Points can be awarded when a shot hits a target and for the shots that went the farthest.

Scouts work together to build their launchers as quickly as possible.

View "Patrol Challenge: Scout Stave Launcher" http://www.programresources.org/scout-stave-launcher-video/

- Freestanding Flagpole Challenge -

Putting Their Heads Together and Using Their SKILLS!

<u>Square Lashing, Roundturn with Two Half Hitches or Rolling Hitch, and Prusik or Rolling Hitch</u> – This challenge affords a definite opportunity for a patrol to put their heads together and figure out how to build the thing.

Materials: six Scout staves, seven 6-foot x 1/4-inch lashing ropes, four light 6-foot guylines, one 15-foot light line

ACTIVITIES

for a halyard, one 3-foot cord to make a top loop for the halyard, two short, pencil-sized sticks to secure the patrol flag to the halyard through existing grommets, a patrol flag for each patrol, freestanding flagpole diagram http://www.programresources.org/wp-content/uploads/2016/02/Self-Standing-Flagpole-Diagram.pdf

Method: With the above materials and some time to plan, patrols are challenged to build a freestanding flagpole capable of raising and lowering their patrol flag.

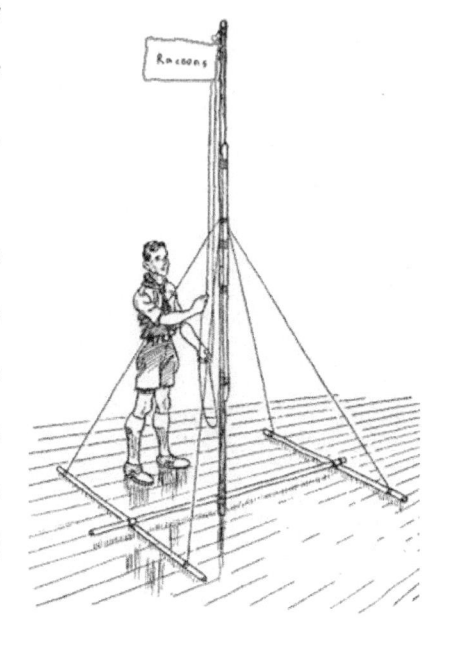

Scoring: Points can be awarded to the patrols who can complete the challenge within the allotted time.

View "Patrol Challenge: Raising a Flagpole http://www.programresources.org/self-standing-flagpole-video/

- Snake Race -

Steady as She Goes!

Shear Lashing – This one's tricky! The key is tying the shear lashings that are tight enough so the snake won't come apart in the middle of trying to complete the challenge. Lots of fun.

Materials: For each patrol: 6 Scout staves, five 6-foot lashing ropes

ACTIVITIES

Method: Patrols line up in parallel formation at a starting line. On signal, the patrol lays out the 6 staves and lashes them together using one, tight shear lashing at each joint. When complete, six patrol members straddle the staves facing the same direction, reach down and grab the chain of staves, then start moving them forward, between their legs. The Scout in front swings the first stave up overhead and passes it back to the Scout behind him. When the last Scout receives the stave passed overhead, he then swings it back down under his legs and starts moving the chain back forward again until the staves are in their original position.

Scoring: The first patrol finished with their "snake" still intact wins.

View "Patrol Challenge: Snake Race" http://www.programresources.org/snake-race-video/

SCOUT PIONEERING — Ol' Fashioned Outdoor Fun!

CHAPTER 6

CAMP GADGETS

"My ideal camp is where everyone is cheery and busy, where the patrols are kept intact under all circumstances, and where every patrol leader and Scout takes a genuine pride in his camp and his gadgets." —
Lord Baden-Powell

A good camp gadget should be durable, aesthetically pleasing, and serve a purpose. From camp tables to dish washing racks, there are many different designs and ideas from which to choose. Perhaps the best are those devised to serve a specific function and created from resources that just happen to be on hand. A perfect example is a flag holder improvised by a

SCOUT PIONEERING — Ol' Fashioned Outdoor Fun!

Timeless Outdoor Skills: two forked sticks and a crossbar suspend an 8-quart pot of water over their cooking fire.

Scout at camp, fashioned by lashing two sections of bamboo to the front upright pole of a dining fly. The top section was simply a hollow cylinder through which the flagpole could easily slip, and the lower section contained an intact internode which served as an ideal stopper. The diameter of the bamboo was just a little larger than the flagpole so it fit just fine. It stayed perfectly upright and the flagpole was easily removed, accessible and portable. It was an ingenious design, and an ideal illustration of Scout engineering!

CAMP GADGETS

Most camp gadgets are suited for longer term, front country camping trips, but they can also be set up for any occasion. All of the materials needed to build these neat, campsite improvements can be carried to the site quite easily.

The following pages contain descriptions and materials for a variety of camp gadgets, many of which are very simple, some of which are more complicated, and all of which are highly functional.

An Variety of Camp Gadgets Assembled throughout the Scoutcraft Area at Scout Camp

- Hand Wash Station -

This wash station is the ideal First Class camp gadget! It's sturdy, portable, and very useful when camping away from washroom facilities. Inherent in its design is a sound approach to a variety of pioneering concepts and skills. When this project's built with all the lashings tight and all the legs, cross-

CAMP GADGETS - Hand Wash Station

bar, and support pieces placed in the proper position and tightly lashed, it stands out as a fine example of a well-engineered and highly functional camp gadget. Each of the three legs making up the tripod get a lashed-on support piece, and the wash station's stability stems from the fact the design contains three triangles.

Working together gets it done fast.

To start, you'll need six good, straight sticks as follows:

- two 2-foot x 3/4 to 1-inch for the leg braces
- two 4-foot x 3/4 to 1-inch for the back leg and crossbar
- two 5-foot x 3/4 to 1-inch for the front legs

SCOUT PIONEERING — Ol' Fashioned Outdoor Fun!

You'll also need need:

- one 10-foot x 1/4-inch manila rope for the tripod lashing
- six 6-foot x 1/4-inch manila ropes for the square lashings
- bar of soap in a sock with a 3-foot cord
- small to medium-sized towel with a 3-foot cord
- No. 10 can or 4-quart pot with a bail

This and several types of camp gadgets can be lashed together simply using binder twine! Just double the suggested lengths and lash simultaneously with double strands.

Hand Wash Station Lashed Together with Binder Twine

CAMP GADGETS - Hand Wash Station

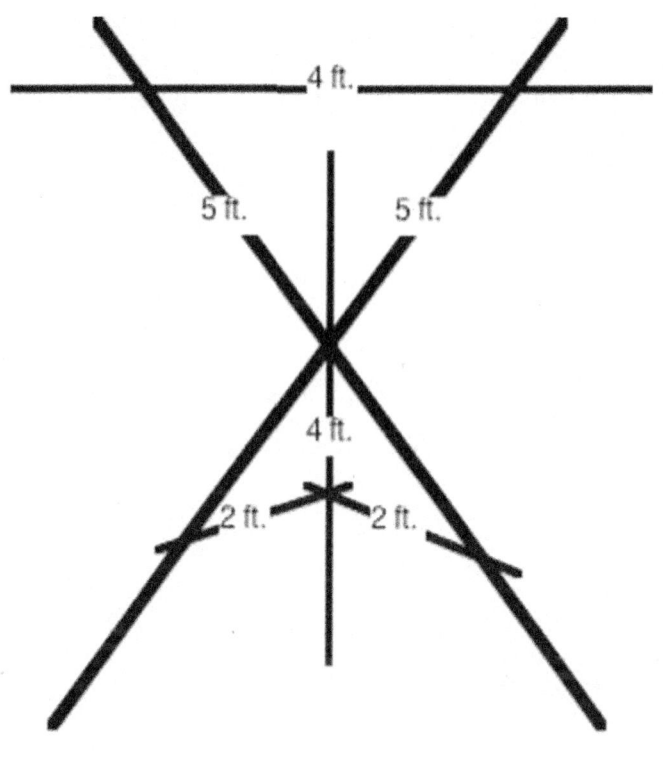

Layout for the Sticks

Here's the assembly procedure.

Make the tripod. Using the 10-foot rope, lash the two 5-foot sticks and one 4-foot stick together with a tight tripod lashing. The 4-foot stick should be in the middle. Make sure the butt ends of all three of these sticks are even to one another.

Separate the legs and set the tripod up. The success of this project relies on a well-tied, *tight* tripod lashing.

Lash on the braces. Using four square lashings, lash one end of the 2-foot sticks to the 5-foot legs and the other end of the 2-foot sticks to the four-foot leg.

Lash on the crossbar. Using two more square lashings, tightly lash the other 4-foot stick to the top extended sections of the two 5-foot sticks to make a crossbar for the towel and soap-in-a-sock.

Add the soap, water, and towel. Tie the end of one 3-foot cord to the soap-in-a-sock and the end of the other 3-foot cord to the towel, and hang them on either side of the 4-foot crossbar.

Hang the can filled with water on the end of the 4-foot stick extending from the front of the tripod. During the camping trip, change the water as necessary. Make sure the soap-in-a-sock is not left in the can after use as it will melt.

One of the beauties of using metal containers is that in cold weather, the can of water can be heated in the fire or over a stove.

CAMP GADGETS - Hand Wash Station

Washing His Hands Before Breakfast on a Cold, Winter Camping Trip

- Fire Bucket Holders -

Single and Double Fire Bucket Holders

In addition to being the height of simplicity, these fire bucket holders make a valuable contribution towards safety around the fire circle. Since it's always a safe bet to have a supply of water right near your cooking and campfires, why not add some convenience and accessibility to the campsite, especially because when fire buckets are on the ground, they're frequently knocked over, inadvertently kicked, and even stepped in!

CAMP GADGETS: Fire Bucket Holders

In this design for a **single fire bucket holder**, a diagonal support brace forming a triangle is what makes it work. Without it, the notched stick would invariably tilt downward from the weight of the filled bucket.

Simple, Single Fire Bucket Holder

Here are the suggested materials:

- one pioneering stake or a 3-foot x 1-inch stick with a point
- two 2-foot x 1-inch straight sticks (one with a notch at one end)
- three 6 to 10-foot x 1/4-inch lashing ropes

The procedure is simple.

1. Where you want the fire bucket, pound in the stake deep enough so it doesn't shake.
2. Lash on the notched stick with a tight square lashing extending out from the stake at a right angle.

3. Near the notch, lash on the support brace at a 90° angle (not *too* tightly) and then position the stick so it intersects with the pounded in stake in such a way that the notched stick extends straight out.

4. Secure this position with a tight square lashing.

Simple Double Fire Bucket Holder

The materials needed for this ultra-simple, **double fire bucket holder** are two pioneering stakes, a solid stick about 30 inches long with a notch on either end to hang the buckets, and two short 1/4-inch manila lashing ropes, 6 to 10 feet long. In a sensible place near the fire circle, pound in the pioneering stakes, approximately two feet apart. Then, making sure the notches on the 30-inch crossbar are facing up, lash it to the two stakes with tight square lashings. Fill the fire buckets and hang them on either side. That's all there is to it. For convenience, the crossbar can be used as a rack to hang additional stuff.

- Scout Stave Camp Table -

This small camp table can be comprised completely of Scout staves. It's 100% functional and provides a convenient raised surface for personal, patrol, or troop use. It's simple design makes it quick and easy to set up, and it's remarkably stable.

Here's a list of materials:

- four Scout staves for the table legs
- good supply of Scout staves for the table top (twelve work great)
- two sturdy 2-1/2-foot sticks (or a Scout stave cut in half)
- one 20-foot rope or cord
- two sturdy stakes

Make the table legs. Start by lashing together four Scout staves into two sets of shear legs with 6-foot manila lashing ropes. Square or shear lashings can be used to join the staves at the top.

Lash on the table top supports. Next, with two square lashings, lash a 2-1/2-foot stick to connect each set of shear legs about 30 inches off the ground. (A Scout stave separated in two is ideal.) This will form two A-frames, one for each side of the table. Make sure each of these support sticks are lashed on straight and at the same distance from the bottom end of both sets of legs.

CAMP GADGETS: Scout Stave Camp Table

Securely hold up the A-frames. This is surely the best part. Find the midpoint of a 20-foot line. About two feet away, tie a Clove Hitch at the top of one of the Scout staves of one of the A-frames. Repeat this process on the other side attaching the line with a Clove Hitch to one of the Scout staves of the opposite A-frame.

Clove Hitches attach the center supporting line to the A-frames.

Secure each end of the 20-foot line to stakes driven into the ground on either side, about 5 feet away, so the line extends out evenly from each end of this table framework. You can use Round Turns with Two Half Hitches, Taut-Line Hitches, or rope tackles. Here's the beauty of this configuration: you can manipulate the distance between the A-frames by adjusting the Clove Hitches, and provide optimum stability to the table by placing a good, reasonable strain on the line at each stake. It will stand up impressively, in a rigid fashion.

Lash on the table top. Finally, lay 12 Scout staves, side by side, on top of the 2-1/2-foot support sticks, and using binder twine, lash them in place with floor lashings.

Left: 12 Scout Staves Form the Table Top / Right: The Scout Stave Camp Table Set Up in a Camp Kitchen

CAMP GADGETS

- Scout Stave Dish Washing Rack -

Drawings for dish washing rack designs are common. But, until you make one and try it with full containers of water, it's difficult to realize what the main challenge really is—to keep the containers from crashing down because they're too heavy! An average plastic wash basin won't have enough of a lip to hold it in place, or is just too flimsy to keep it's shape when filled with water. That's why lashing together a framework alone usually won't suffice. Therefore, in addition to the framework, this design includes a platform made up of two bottom basin support staves for the basins to rest upon. This successfully addresses the weight issue.

Scouts are Introduced to the Scout Stave Dish Washing Rack in the Pioneering Village at the National Jamboree

The next challenge is one that's common to many a pioneering structure, be it large or small. How do we keep the rack itself from falling over? You overcome this basic concern by bringing into play the same stability solution used in making the Scout Stave Camp Table. It's exactly the same concept that keeps a monkey bridge erect. Like the Scout Stave Camp Table, we connect two upright A-frames with a rope, and using the same rope, we anchor them securely in place on either side. Here's what you'll need:

- ten Scout staves
- fourteen 6-foot x 1/4-inch lashing ropes
- one 20-foot rope or cord
- two sturdy stakes
- three 18 quart wash basins with a grip lip around the top

Make the A-frames. Because the rack will be holding around nine gallons of water, approximately 72 pounds, the lashings for this project need to be especially tight. An easy way to assure you'll have well-lashed A-frames is to first square lash the tops at 90° and then the ledger to one leg, also at 90°. When the other leg and the other end of the ledger are brought together for lashing, this will create some strain on the lashings yielding a nice tight A-frame. (Careful it's not *too* tight, and of course, if you so desire, you can always start with a shear lashing at the top, or just square lash all three legs at the same time.)

Make two identical A-frames like so.

Lash the ledger in place about 28 inches from the top of the legs. Since all we're using are Scout Staves, in this design one side of the ledger can purposely extend out much farther than the other on each A-frame—a place to hang some towels (or whatever).

Connect the A-frames and stand them up. Where you want the rack to be located, hammer in two stakes about 12 feet apart, and position the A-frames between. Halve the 20-foot rope or cord and approximating the midpoint between the

CAMP GADGETS: Scout Stave Dishwashing Rack

A-frames, secure the rope to the top of one leg with a Clove Hitch, about 2 feet from the middle of the line. Pulling the rope to the other A-frame, repeat the process on the top of a leg on the other side.

The A-Frames Connected and Standing with a Line that is
Clove Hitched to the Tops of Each

Tie the ends of the rope to the stakes on either side. As with the Scout Stave Camp Table, you can use Round Turns with Two Half Hitches, Taut-Line Hitches, or rope tackles.

Add the Side Basin Support Staves. Tightly lash a stave to the outside of the legs of each A-frame, about 20 inches from the top. The front and back edges of the wash basins will rest on these side basin support staves. Use a basin to aid in assuring the pairs of legs are the right distance, so the front and back edges of the basins will fit nicely on the rack and lay properly. As necessary, make any adjustments.

Add the two bottom basin support staves. The A-frame ledgers will now serve to do something more than keep the legs of the A-frames from shifting. They'll now also support the two remaining staves that assure the basins stay put! Lash these two staves parallel to one another on top of the ledgers, on either side of the rack. Use the basins to help measure their distance apart.

Place the basins on the rack. Once you check to see all the lashings are tight, and the central rope is secure and stabilizing the structure, then you're ready to bring on the basins. Position them side by side and fill them about 3/4 of the

CAMP GADGETS: Scout Stave Dishwashing Rack

way up with the proper temperature of water for washing, rinsing, and sanitizing.

Making Dish Washing More Enjoyable

SCOUT PIONEERING — Ol' Fashioned Outdoor Fun!

- Tool Racks -

Left: Tool Rack 1 / Right: Tool Rack 2

Fundamentally speaking, as long as a campsite is safe and clean, all's well. However, especially for longer term camps (or when displaying demonstrations of Scoutcraft skills), there's definitely something to say for the added convenience of a campsite tool rack. Set up in a prominent location, e.g. in or near an axe yard, a tool rack serves as a reminder to put tools back where they belong. A place for everything, and everything in its place, especially wood tools, goes a long way in keeping things well-organized and limiting accidents.

CAMP GADGETS: Tool Racks

A Scout replaces a mallet in a Tool Rack 1 made with four Scout staves.

Tool Rack 1 – Construction is very simple. Basically, all that's needed are four poles; two 6-foot uprights, and two 5-foot cross pieces work fine. Four Scout staves will also perfectly fill the bill. The cross pieces are connected to the uprights with four square lashings.

Tools are hung on the rack, held in place by looped cords attached to the cross pieces with Lark's Heads.

When it's not practical to pound the upright poles into the ground, an effective option is to solidly drive in a couple of pioneering stakes up against the poles where they will be standing. Then, to hold the uprights securely in a vertical position, lash the poles firmly to the stakes with a couple of tight round lashings.

Scouts tie two round lashings to join the upright poles to the stakes.

Tool Rack 2 – The main difference between Tool Rack 1 and Tool Rack 2 is in Tool Rack 1 all the tools are hung suspended by a cord from the upper cross piece with the handles resting against the lower cross piece. In Tool Rack 2, the tools' handles are slipped in between two parallel cross pieces. This way, they're held very nicely in place and any shifting or wobbling around that might be experienced in Tool Rack 1 is eliminated. In order to slip the tools between the two parallel cross pieces, the diameter of the two uprights needs to be a little larger than the diameter of the thickest handle of any tool you'll be hanging.

When you're ready to lash on the cross pieces, lash on the first higher than the longest tool. It needs to be at a height easy enough to comfortably place the tools on and take the tools off the rack, without needing to reach up too high or bend over. Secure the first cross piece in front of the uprights with a couple of tight square lashings, and then secure the second cross piece to the

Two Cross Pieces Lashed to an Upright

uprights in exactly the same position, but on the other side of the uprights. You'll be tying a tight square lashing here too, and there's plenty of room to wrap and frap. That's all there is to it.

SCOUT PIONEERING — Ol' Fashioned Outdoor Fun!

A Scout replaces the mallet in a Tool Rack 2

CAMP GADGETS: Tool Racks

If you'd like to erect a cover over the tool rack, you can lash another cross piece to the very tops of longer uprights, and rig up a tarp, using this third cross piece as a ridge pole.

Tool Rack 2 With an Improvised Cover

- Scout Stave Flagpole -

A Scout Stave Flagpole is put up for a troop meeting opening ceremony.

Flags engender pride! Flying 'em high is great for Scout spirit, and making a 15-foot flagpole is really easy. All you need are four Scout staves, six 6-foot lashing ropes, three 15-foot guylines, and three stakes.

CAMP GADGETS: Scout Stave Flagpole

The main key to *making* a simple flagpole out of Scout staves is round lashings and knowing where to tie them. The space where the two poles are joined, gets two tight round lashings—one on either side of the overlap and right near the ends of each stave. When using four Scout staves, you can simply overlap them about 10 inches.

The main key to *raising and securing* a simple flagpole is tying on three guylines about 3/4 of the way up, and extending them out equidistant from one another. The stakes should form an equilateral triangle.

15 Foot Scout Stave Flagpole

While the flagpole is being lashed together, a Scout or Scouts can go about putting the stakes in the ground, pacing out the proper distance and hammering them in at the correct angle with the notches in the proper position. Before raising the pole, the three guylines should be tied on using Round Turns with Two Half Hitches or Rolling Hitches. Then, with one Scout holding the flagpole erect, three Scouts can each take a guyline and attach it to a stake with a tight Taut-Line Hitch. (Because this is a 15-foot flagpole and is made of lightweight Scout staves, Taut-Line Hitches will suffice. For heavier poles, more substantial anchors and rope tackles or Roundturns with Two Half Hitches are needed.)

The flag can be tied onto the top stave before raising the pole, or if desired, a simple 30-foot halyard can be added by tying a ring to the very top.

With practice, a Scout patrol can make and erect the 15-foot Scout Stave Flagpole in a few short minutes.

View "Raising a Flagpole (Demonstration)" Video http://www.programresources.org/flagpole-race-demo-video/

CAMP GADGETS

- Clothes Drying Rack -

You've got to love this design. It's compact, sturdy, and ingenious!

This drying rack is based on suspending two concentric, equilateral triangles to make six cross sections for hanging wet clothing or towels during a long term encampment. Of course,

191

if there's a practical need, there's no reason it can't be built on an overnighter.

A very clever camp gadget, it takes up less space while drying more wet things. It also eliminates the clutter of clothing and towels haphazardly strewn around on tables, tree branches, tent platforms, or overcrowded on a disorganized array of drooping clothes lines. It can be set up in a location where there is the most sunshine, and is especially useful when camping in an open area with few trees.

A Clothes Drying Rack Set up in an Open Field

CAMP GADGETS: Clothes Drying Rack

Materials (adapt these as you like)

- three 4-foot x 1-inch sticks
- three 5-foot x 1-inch sticks (Scout staves are ideal)
- one 6-foot x 1-1/2 to 2-1/2-inch straight pole for the upright center pole (another Scout stave does the trick)
- one 30-inch pioneering stake
- eight 6-foot x 1/4-inch manila lashing ropes
- three 15-foot support lines
- three sturdy stakes

Lash the triangles. Start by lashing together two equilateral triangles, one smaller for the top (three 4-foot sticks), and the larger one for the bottom (three 5-foot staves). Use square lashings. One easy way is to lash two at 90° and then bend them in and tie the third square lashing to make the triangle. This yields a nice, tightly-lashed triangle. (Be careful you're not putting *too* much stress on the ropes and poles when preparing to apply the third lashing.)

Erect the upright. Pound in the pioneering stake where you want the rack to stand and lash on the center pole securely with two tight round lashings. Making this upright stand up vertically without moving or wobbling at all is a key to a good and sturdy clothes dryer. So, solidly drive in the stake and make sure it's as straight as possible. Also, make sure the round lashings are well-tied and tight.

Three Support Lines Connected to the Center Pole with Rolling Hitches

Attach the triangles to the center pole. Lay the triangles on the ground over the upright, first the larger triangle, and then the smaller one on top. Tie the three 15-foot support lines to the top of the center pole with Rolling Hitches or Roundturns with Two Half Hitches. Tie each corner of the smaller triangle to a support line so it will be suspended about 4-1/2 feet above the ground. Use Clove Hitches, which can be adjusted as necessary to assure the triangle hangs evenly and the 4-foot sticks are horizontal. Continuing with each of the three support lines, repeat this process for the larger triangle so it will hang about 3-1/2 to 4 feet above the ground.

CAMP GADGETS: Clothes Drying Rack

Anchor the support lines. Hammer in a small stake a foot or so out, in line with each corner of the bottom triangle. Using the remaining length of the support lines, attach them to the stakes with a simple Taut-Line Hitch. This will further stabilize the clothes dryer and enable you to make fine-tuned adjustments to the way the triangles lay.

A view of Clove Hitches at the corners of two triangles, and a Taut-Line Hitch connected to the stake.

Easy Alternative – *An alternative approach to supporting the center pole is to double the function of the support lines, utilizing them also as guylines!* This is the same fundamental approach that comes into play and is so effective when putting up a flagpole. In this case, the position of the stakes already form an equilateral triangle. By driving them in 4 feet further away from the center pole, the support lines don't merely stabilize the triangles, but also keep the whole structure erect.

SCOUT PIONEERING — Ol' Fashioned Outdoor Fun!

In the same way a flagpole can be secured in an upright position by utilizing three guylines, the above clothes drying rack's center pole is a Scout stave held erect by the support lines, doubling as guylines.

- Freestanding Trash Bag Holder -

Getting that trash bag off the ground has all kinds of advantages. When you can drive three or four sticks into the ground, it's easy to hitch on a bag at the tops. But, there might be any number of reasons why hammering in sticks isn't possible. The ground's got too many rocks. The ground *is* rock. You're in a parking lot or on the sidewalk during a fundraiser. You're indoors.

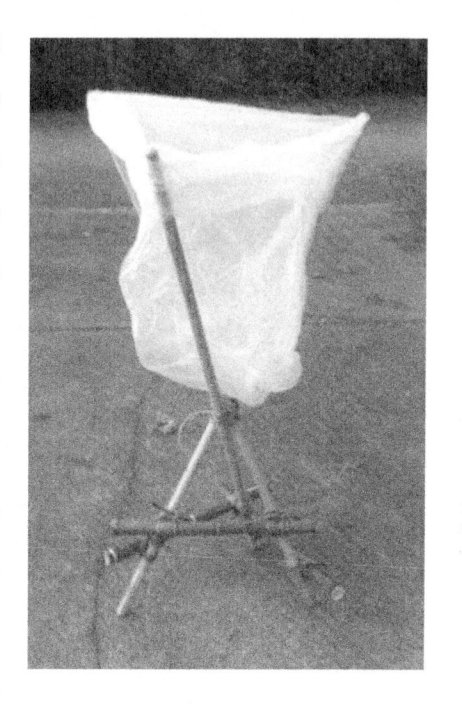

In these cases, to hold up a trash bag (when there is no trash can), you can simply lash three Scout staves or similar poles into a tripod and lash on some short cross pieces to keep it stable. All that's required are seven lashing ropes, one for a tripod lashing and six for square lashings. For the poles you need three 4 to 5-foot sticks for the tripod legs, and three short sticks for the tripod leg supports.

With this gadget, the tripod lashing is tied below the middle of the longer sticks.

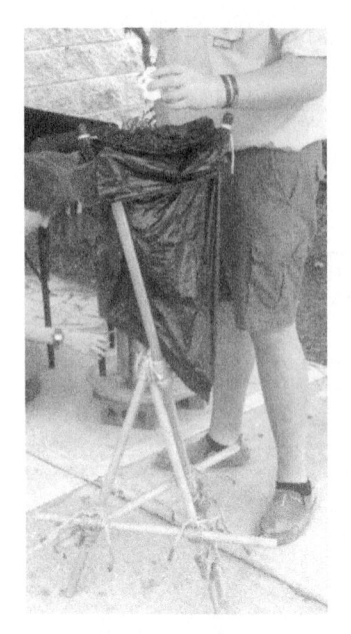

Trash Bag Holder Set Up on a Concrete Terrace

The length that the sticks extend on top of the lashing will be determined by the size of the bag your holding. Also, to secure the bag on the holder, and too shorten or lengthen the amount the bag hangs, you can fold the top of the bag over the three upper leg extensions as much or as little as you like.

CHAPTER 7

SAFE PIONEERING

In and through the challenges, fun, and rewards that go hand in hand with Scout Pioneering, there can be no substitute for prudent behavior and common sense. As you begin your pioneering activities, safety must be your first consideration. The following safety points are some that you and your group should keep in mind:

1. Before and after each use, check all equipment, ropes, poles, tools, and hardware to ensure they are in good working condition.
2. All equipment should be treated with respect and used appropriately for its intended purpose.
3. Appoint a safety officer who, along with the rest of the group, should constantly check the work site to keep it clean of debris. Equipment should be kept in an organized fashion before, during, and after its use.
4. During the construction of a project, only one person should give instructions and signals.

SAFE PIONEERING

5. There should always be plenty of room between the person carrying spars and people around them.
6. Do not work during rainy or wet conditions. Rope and spars become slippery, as does your footing.
7. Wear clothing to fit the season and wear gloves when necessary to protect your hands. Work smart and don't lift more than you can handle.
8. Spars resting on the ground are not for standing upon. They can unexpectedly roll causing injuries.
9. When lifting a spar to facilitate the frapping of a tripod or shear lashing, care should always be taken to ensure the person working the rope doesn't injure their fingers.
10. Take regular breaks to discuss the work in progress and ensure that everyone understands what is required of them.
11. Take extra care when pounding in pioneering stakes.
12. For added safety, heel in the legs of a structure from 4 to 6 inches.
13. If the design calls for a certain size and type of rope or spar, do not substitute something of lesser strength.
14. Before allowing general use, run a complete test to see everything is working correctly.

Like with this Single A-Frame Bridge they built at the national jamboree, Scouts should only climb on a structure they make after it's been completely inspected.

15. Keep checking all anchors on the pioneering project as strain is applied during use.
16. The number of people using a platform should be strictly limited to the maximum number established beforehand and announced by the safety officer.
17. There should only be one person on a monkey bridge at a time.

SAFE PIONEERING

Raising any tall structure requires all hands on deck—some lifting, some hoisting, and some with lines to assure the project isn't over-pulled. The appointed safety officer needs to be alert to call out the signals and oversee the operation.

18. Jumping or playing around while on a structure is unacceptable. Scouts should only climb on board certain projects after all lashings are tight, and the structure has been completely inspected.

19. While crossing a monkey bridge, people shouldn't bounce or purposely swing or sway on the ropes, nor should anyone race to see how quickly they can get across.

SCOUT PIONEERING — Ol' Fashioned Outdoor Fun!

20. Those waiting their turn to cross a monkey bridge should stay off the ropes between the anchors and the A-frames.
21. Everyone should stay completely off a monkey bridge whenever the foot and hand ropes are being tightened, or the spanner ropes are being adjusted.
22. When the day's work is complete, untie all knots, coil all ropes, check all hardware, and store everything in its proper place.

A Boy Scout is attentive to the safety of the Cub Scouts crossing the monkey bridge.

PROJECT BUILDING

CHAPTER 8

PROJECT BUILDING

Large Patrol-sized Raft Built During a Weekend Outing

Just like pioneering skills, there are numerous pioneering projects! This chapter features most of our favorites.

Woodbadge training at Gilwell always used to include a full day of pioneering and the three main projects were towers, bridges and *raft*s. To start things off, here are some thoughts about building rafts.

Raft building stands out as one of the most fun-filled and potentially exhilarating Scout Pioneering activities. It incorporates all the planning, preparation, and Scout engineering that contribute to the richness of the pioneering experience, and when the structure can actually float and carry the participants involved, the pronounced element of happy success inherent in the process is undeniable.

Through the years, raft building has played a major role in pioneering activities, and thanks to the often hilarious escapades of John Thurman during his extended term as Camp Chief at Gilwell, riding on a raft one has designed and built has become a part of a rich and rewarding Scout Pioneering heritage. Nothing provides the same kind of challenge and fun as using the materials on hand to build one, and then embarking on a one of a kind adventure across a lake with your friends.

Three Original Designs Using 30-Gallon Drums

A modern-day source of flotation are large plastic drums. John Thurman never provided any clues regarding how to lash

Lashing on a 55 Gallon Drum to the Underside of the Framework

drums onto the framework, though he did suggest that each one should receive a separate lashing. That way, if one drum was to come loose, losing it wouldn't be the cause of an "unfortunate" chain reaction. Naturally, the bung holes should be positioned as high as possible and care should be taken that everything is lashed tightly.

Another good rule of thumb is to first lash on the drums to the underside of the raft between poles that are spaced in such a way that the drums cannot pop through. Once this is accomplished, the procedure is to turn the raft right side up and then complete the building process.

Creativity, and ingenuity come into play during the planning and preparation phases of raft building. When it's time to position the materials, lash things together, get it in the water, and get it moving with everybody on board, what also comes into play is an extra degree of teamwork and cooperation.

PROJECT BUILDING

Flipping Over the Framework

Sink or swim, raft building and then, hopefully, raft riding is great fun. It's just about impossible not to have a fantastic time!

View "Large Patrol Raft" https://youtu.be/wqTqAfdcuiM

- Double A-Frame Monkey Bridge -

The well-known, traditional monkey bridge is perhaps the most familiar of all Scout Pioneering projects, and is often a central attraction at public gatherings where Scouting is represented. This double A-frame approach to building a monkey bridge, designed by Scout Pioneering Legend, Adolph Peschke has many advantages:

PROJECT BUILDING: Double A-Frame Monkey Bridge

- The materials can be managed without difficulty by Scout-age youth.
- The double A-frame provides a wider base making it less likely to tip over.
- The positions of the A-frames can be adjusted so the span between the hand ropes can be narrowed for better balance as you make the crossing.

Here's a list of materials:

- eight 8-foot x 4-inch A-frame legs
- four 6-foot x 3-inch ledgers
- fourteen 15-foot x 1/4-inch lashing ropes for square lashings
- two 50-foot x 1/2-inch hand ropes
- one 50-foot x 1/2-inch or 3/4-inch foot rope
- five to seven 8-foot x 1/4-inch stringer ropes
- six 10-foot x 1/4-inch lashing ropes for round lashings
- six pioneering stakes for each 3-2-1 anchor
- (eight pioneering stakes for each log-and-stake anchor)
- (one 4-foot x 5-inch spar for each log-and-stake anchor)
- two 10-foot x 1/2-inch polypropylene ropes for rope grommets
- two 3-inch x 1/2-inch welded rings
- two pieces of scrap canvas or burlap for foot rope saddles
- binder twine and small stakes for anchor tieback straps

What follows are the various steps, all of which need to be completed before the bridge is done. But, there needn't be a set order. As with many pioneering projects, a pioneering crew can be divided into subcrews, and a variety of tasks can be attended to at the same time.

Two Crews Each Working on Separate Subassemblies

PROJECT BUILDING: Double A-Frame Monkey Bridge

Make the A-frames. With tight square lashings, build four identical A-frames. A tape measure can be used to make sure the position of the spars match and the lashings will be applied where the poles intersect at the same distance for each A-frame. Another approach is to lay out two legs and a ledger on the ground in position for lashing. Then, drive a stake in the ground where both legs and the ledger intersect, and where the legs cross at the top. Use these three stakes as a template for lashing together all four A-frames.

Making Four Identical A-Frames

Join the A-frames. When the four identical A-frames are built, join them together into two double A-frames. This can be accomplished by laying an A-frame on the ground and then placing another on top, so that the bottom ledgers overlap one-half their length (approximately 3 feet). The ledgers of each A-frame should face each other so they touch. If there are enough crew members, you can first stand the A-frames up and then position them. Where the legs cross, at the X formed by one leg from each A-frame, join them together with a good, tight square lashing.

Turning Single A-Frames Into Double A-Frames

The point where these two legs are lashed together is where the foot rope will rest. You can adjust the overlap of the two A-frames which will determine how high the foot rope will be off the ground. Also note where the tops of the A-frames are, because this is where the hand ropes will be.

Finally, lash the two bottom ledgers together where they overlap with three, secure round lashings.

PROJECT BUILDING: Double A-Frame Monkey Bridge

Layout the site. Before you can position the double A-frames, the site needs to be laid out. Stretch a 20-foot length of binder twine, cord, or rope along the center line of where the monkey bridge is to be built. Mark the center point for later reference. From the center, measure 10 feet toward each end. This is where the A-frames are to be placed. They should be 20 feet apart. Then mark out another 10 feet from each A-frame to where the anchors are to be built.

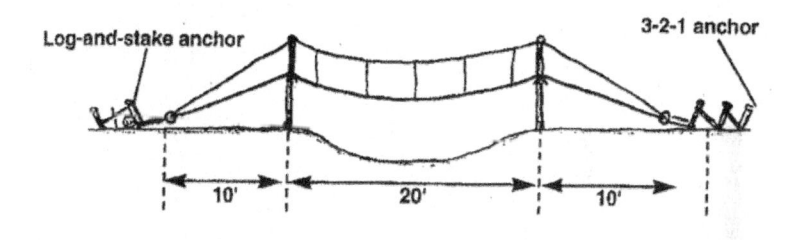

Diagram from Adolph's Edition of the Pioneering Merit Badge Pamphlet

These dimensions are for building a bridge that spans 20 feet. When using 50-foot hand and foot ropes, 20 feet should be the maximum distance between each double A-frame. The extra 30 feet of rope is needed to have 15 feet of rope at each end so there's a 10-foot distance between the A-frames and their anchors, and another 5 feet for the appropriate knots.

Build the anchors. The foot and hand ropes will be attached to anchors at both ends. Unless natural anchors are available, build a 3-2-1 anchor, or a log-and-stake anchor, 10 feet from where the A-frames will be erected.

Building a 3-2-1 Anchor

Rope grommet – After the pioneering stakes are pounded in, attach a rope grommet with a ring in it.

Position the A-frames. Prepare to erect the monkey bridge by moving the completed double A-frames into position no more than 20 feet apart. Once the double A-frames are placed at the location for the bridge, make sure the butt ends of all the legs are resting solidly on level ground.

PROJECT BUILDING: Double A-Frame Monkey Bridge

Hand and foot ropes – Lay the foot rope in a straight line off to the side of where the A-frames are laying. Then line up the two hand ropes on the ground next to each other so both hand ropes are parallel to the foot rope and 42 inches away.

Stringer ropes – Now you can add the stringer ropes that will go from the foot rope to the hand ropes. Start by attaching an 8-foot long stringer rope at the center of the foot rope, with a simple roundturn. The stringer is attached to the foot rope so that both ends are 4 feet long. Tie one end of the stringer rope to one of the hand ropes with a Clove Hitch. Then do the same with the other end of the stringer rope, attaching it to the other hand rope. Add two more stringer ropes on both sides of the center stringer rope, tying them about 4 feet apart. If desired, additional stringer ropes can be added.

Optional 4-foot ladder rungs can be lashed onto the A-frames at each end of the bridge for easier climbing on and off.

Assemble the bridge. You're just about ready to assemble the bridge. First place a piece of heavy cloth, called a "saddle," in the V formed by both double A-frames. This will protect the foot rope and allow it to slide a little in the V without interfering with the lashing rope.

Now get the crew together to erect the bridge. You will need a safety officer to watch for any problems that might occur, and a signal caller to tell the crew members what to do. You will need two Scouts to lift and hold each double A-frame in place, two more Scouts to lift the foot rope into the V of the double A-frames, and two more Scouts to lift the two hand ropes into place at the tops of the A-frames. Lift everything into place. Then, holding the A-frames steady, temporarily tie the hand and foot ropes into the rings of the grommets using a Roundturn with Two Half Hitches.

Forming a Rope Tackle in the Foot Rope

Tighten the foot rope. Now you can put a strain on the foot rope. Configure a rope tackle at each end which, when tightened by one Scout, is an

PROJECT BUILDING: Double A-Frame Monkey Bridge

excellent procedure to maintain the optimum foot rope tension, and an easy-to-use remedy for too much sagging due to repeated, heavy use and over stretching. As soon as the bridge is used a few times, there will be a sag in the rope. This is fine because it means you're working with reduced strain on the foot rope as a safety measure.

Tighten the hand ropes. Next, tie the hand ropes to the top ends of the A-frames. First, loosen one end at a time from the anchors. Then, with a couple of underhand loops, form a Clove Hitch to tie the hand rope to the top end of one leg of the double A-frame. As you're tying these Clove Hitches, adjust the strain on the sections of the hand ropes between the double A-frames to match the sag of the foot rope. Also, adjust and even out the stringer ropes so they're evenly spaced and angled properly between the foot rope and both hand ropes. After the hand ropes are tied to the tops of the A-frames, move down and retie the ends of the hand ropes to the rings in the grommets using a Roundturn with Two Half Hitches.

During operation, if the tension on the foot rope has to be tightened, the angle of the stringers might have to be adjusted to keep them lined up evenly on the hand ropes.

Alternatively, the stringer ropes can be tied on after the hand and foot ropes are connected.

Alternative approach – After the anchors are built, stand up both positioned double A-frames and extend the foot rope so it lays evenly over the V where the legs of the A-frames intersect. Place a cushioning cloth saddle over the square lashing, under the foot rope. Pull the line taut and temporarily tie off each end of the foot rope to the ring in the rope grommets. Next, add each hand rope so they extend evenly on both sides. Pulling the line taut, attach the hand ropes to a leg

PROJECT BUILDING: Double A-Frame Monkey Bridge

of each A-frame with an open-ended Clove Hitch. Secure each end to the ring in the rope grommet using a Roundturn with Two Half Hitches. The stringer ropes can now be tied on.

Final testing – With caution, one crew member can get on the bridge as all lashings, anchors, and knots are observed by the safety officer and all other crew members. Make adjustments as required. Safe operation calls for only one Scout to be on the foot rope of the monkey bridge at a time.

View "Double A-Frame Monkey Bridge" https://youtu.be/zLucGXSQT1A

- Double Tripod Chippewa Kitchen -

Chippewa Kitchens come in many shapes and sizes. This version is the ultimate camp kitchen pioneering project, making a wide range of camp cooking operations more convenient. It provides a raised surface for food preparation, a place to hang pans, Dutch Ovens, tools and utensils, a framework from which pots can be safely suspended over a cooking fire, and primarily,

PROJECT BUILDING: Double Tripod Chippewa Kitchen

a very convenient, raised surface for cooking with hot coals. The double tripod design yields a stable structure, and the size of the cooking area can be varied in accordance with the size of the spars you choose. Scaled down versions work well for a single patrol.

Materials needed for the full-sized kitchen:

- two 8 or 10-foot x 3-inch platform support spars
- six 8-foot x 3-inch tripod leg spars
- two 6-foot x 3-inch front tripod braces
- four 6-foot x 2-1/2-inch side tripod braces
- twenty to forty 3 to 4-foot x 2-inch platform spars
- sixteen 15-foot x 1/4-inch lashing ropes
- two 20-foot x 1/4-inch lashing ropes
- binder twine
- burlap or canvas
- mineral soil

What follows is a procedure to construct a full-sized, Double Tripod Chippewa Kitchen:

Checking Out a Chippewa Kitchen at the National Jamboree

Building the Tripods – Lay three 8-foot tripod legs side by side and lash them together with a *tight* tripod lashing. Make sure the butt ends are at the bottom and even. (If your kitchen will be staying up for an extended period, make the wraps with racking turns.) Stand the tripod up by crossing the *outside* legs underneath the *middle* leg. Repeat this process for the second tripod.

Lashing on the Tripod Braces – Connect the two outside legs with one of the front 6-foot tripod braces. With square lashings, lash the brace so it is perpendicular to the

PROJECT BUILDING: Double Tripod Chippewa Kitchen

ground and 3 feet high. This brace will support the cooking platform, so make sure it's lashed on securely.

Lash a 6-foot side tripod brace to each outside leg and connect them to the middle leg with square lashings, about 2 feet and 2-1/2 feet high respectively.

Repeat this process for the second tripod, making sure the front tripod brace connecting the outside legs is again, 3 feet high.

Positioning the Tripods – Place the tripods so the 6-foot front tripod braces (the ones that are 3 feet off the ground) are facing each other. These braces are the ones that will hold up the long platform support spars, which in turn will support the cooking platform. The distance between the two tripods should be close enough so the long platform support spars can extend over each brace by at least 6 inches.

Lashing on the Platform Support Spars – Place the long platform support spars parallel to each other on top of the three-foot-high tripod brace, on each tripod. Space them apart so the shortest platform spar will extend over their edges by 4 inches on either side. (This will determine whether they'll get lashed on the inside or the outside of the legs.) With four tight square lashings, lash them firmly in place.

Scouts apply Two Floor Lashings for the Platform Spars

Lashing on the Platform Spars – The cooking surface is made up of 3 to 4-foot x 2-inch platform spars, depending on how wide a cooking area will be required. With floor lashings,

PROJECT BUILDING: Double Tripod Chippewa Kitchen

attach them onto the parallel platform supports using binder twine.

Preparing the Cooking Surface – Prior to adding mineral soil, and to keep the soil from falling though the spaces between the platform spars, spread pieces of burlap or canvas over the platform. Finally, cover the platform with a thick layer of mineral soil to protect the platform spars from the intense heat that will be generated from the coals during cooking.

A Chippewa Kitchen Rigged with a Tarp Covering

View "Chippewa Kitchen" https://youtu.be/ttOG0msK4EQ

SCOUT PIONEERING — Ol' Fashioned Outdoor Fun!

Top: Preparing the Coals / Bottom: Serving a Meal Steamed in Foil Packets

PROJECT BUILDING

- Two Basic Subassemblies -

Left: Trestle / Right: Bridge Walkways

Pioneering structures are often comprised of different parts that are assembled independently from one another. For example, in the Double A-Frame Monkey Bridge there are four A-frames, and in the Double Tripod Chippewa kitchen there are two tripods. These separate parts are called subassemblies. After they're built, they're joined together and make up the completed project. The two important subassemblies described on the following pages are the trestle and the bridge walkway.

TRESTLE – In addition to serving as a basic subassembly that adds structural integrity to many pioneering projects, a trestle is the central component for building a variety of bridges where it's used to support the walkways.

The trestle consists of two legs, two ledgers, and two cross braces. When building a bridge, the top ledger is also called a transom. This is the part that supports the walkways. As Adolph Peschke describes, when building a trestle, there is a specific process that can be applied:

To make a trestle, the two ledgers are lashed near the top and bottom of the legs and the cross braces are added, lashing them to the legs. All together, a trestle is composed of nine lashings. Traditionally, eight of them are square lashings and one is a diagonal lashing, which is used to lash the two cross braces together where they cross in the center. A Mark II Square Lashing can also be used where the cross braces intersect, because the completion of the first wrap serves to provide the same action of springing the diagonals together where they cross as the Timber Hitch does with a traditional diagonal lashing, or the Lark's Head does with the Filipino Diagonal Lashing.

PROJECT BUILDING: Two Basic Subassemblies

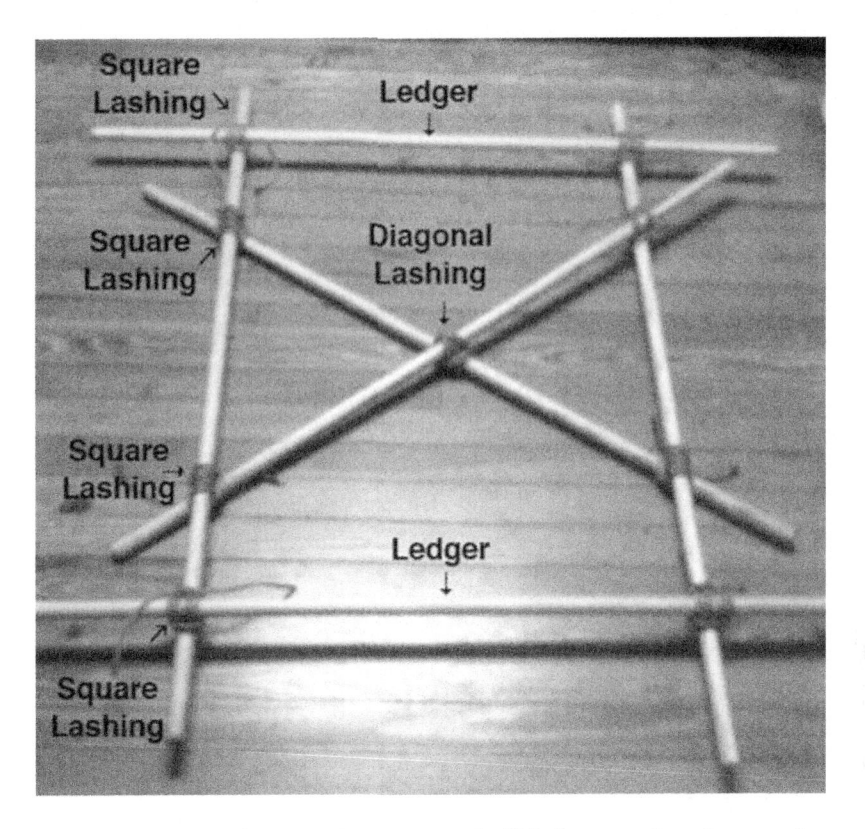

[Figure: Trestle subassembly with labels — Square Lashing, Ledger, Square Lashing, Diagonal Lashing, Square Lashing, Ledger, Square Lashing]

Legs – When setting out to build the trestle, choose the two spars for the legs first. These spars can be most any length, depending on the type and height of the structure you're building. Lay the two legs on the ground with the two butt ends of the spars at the same end and even with one another. Then add the ledgers.

Ledgers – The ledgers are spars that are typically 2 inches to 2-1/2 inches in diameter. The position of the ledgers on the legs will depend on the structure you're building. There are a couple of general rules to keep in mind:

- Always keep the butt ends of the legs even with each other.
- Except in the case where the tops of two trestles will be interlocked, always keep the legs parallel as you're lashing on the ledgers.
- All lashings should be tightly tied, and when building a bridge, make sure the larger, top ledger (transom) is tied most tightly.

Cross Braces – Next, the cross braces are added. The cross braces are spars that are usually 2 inches in diameter. They are lashed to the legs in a particular sequence:

Flip the trestle over and work on the opposite side from the ledgers.

1. Lash one cross brace to the back side of both legs.
2. Lash the bottom end of the second cross brace on the same side as both ends of the first cross brace.
3. Lash the other end on the front side—the side with the ledgers. This is done so that the cross braces are standing

PROJECT BUILDING: Two Basic Subassemblies

slightly apart. There will be a gap where they cross at the center.

After the ends of the ledgers and the cross braces are lashed to the legs, stand the trestle up on end. Adjust the trestle so that the legs are parallel. Also check to see that the top ledger is parallel to the ground. If it is not, lower the trestle, untie the lashing, and adjust it.

Center Lashing – When the legs are parallel and the top ledger is parallel to the ground, you're ready to tie a diagonal or Mark II Square Lashing to the cross braces while the trestle is standing upright. This lashing is very important to the strength of the trestle. Along with springing the two cross braces together, this lashing creates triangles that are important to stiffen the arrangement of the spars and to keep the trestle from racking.

WALKWAYS – The Single A-Frame, Single Trestle, and Single Lock Bridges all consist of two constructed walkways, one extending from either side of a separately-assembled support. (Longer bridges can have additional walkways lashed to additional supports.) For each of these three bridge designs, the same type of walkway can be used. Each walkway can be 10 feet long and consists of two lateral spars and several cross spars. A 10-foot length of 10-inch x 2-inch construction lumber can be added as the plank to walk on.

To make a 10 foot section of walkway, select two 10-foot spars with a butt diameter of 3-1/2 inches. As Adolph describes, these spars should be matched in the amount of sag they have

PROJECT BUILDING: Two Basic Subassemblies

when you stand on them with the ends supported above the ground. If one spar sags more than the other, it will cause the walkway to slant from side to side, making it hard to walk on.

It's practical to save the matched lateral spars to be used for walkways only.

Cross spars – The cross spars for the walkway should be approximately 2 to 2-1/2 inches in diameter and 3 feet long. You'll need two additional cross spars that are 3-1/2 feet long for each walkway section. (The longer spars go at each end of the walkway.)

All of the cross spars are lashed to the lateral spars with 1/4-inch manila. Since the lashing is made only to hold the cross spars in position and not support weight, you can

Lashing on the Walkway Cross Spars

SCOUT PIONEERING — Ol' Fashioned Outdoor Fun!

use a double strand of binder twine as a substitution for the manila.

If you use binder twine, double it over and twist it a few times before you start the lashing. Make sure you have enough to complete the full lashing with the doubled-over binder twine. If you run short, don't finish the lashing with only one strand. Instead, tie on more binder twine to complete the lashing. Each of the cross spars is lashed to the lateral spars with a square lashing, making three wraps and two fraps.

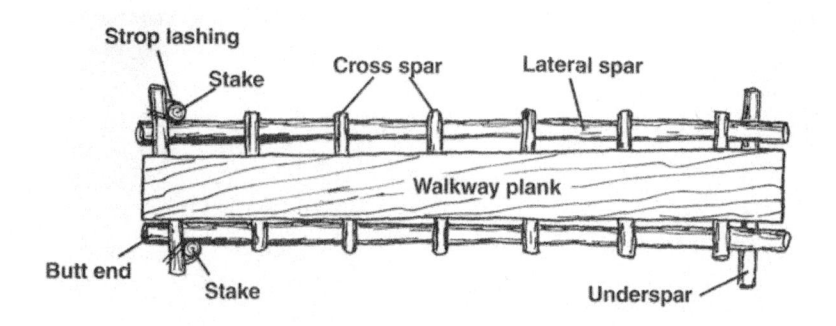

There are two ways to approach adding on the cross spars. If you are going to have a plank over the top of the cross spars, you will need a total of eight cross spars for each walkway. That is, six 3-foot cross spars, and two 3-1/2-foot cross spars. If you are going to walk directly on the cross

PROJECT BUILDING: Two Basic Subassemblies

spars (with no plank on top), you will need enough cross spars to make a safe walkway—one that your foot can't slip through.

Start by lashing one of the 3-1/2-foot cross spars about 6 inches from the butt end of the lateral spars. Place this spar on top of the lateral spars so the ends of the cross spar extend 3 to 4 inches out over both sides of the lateral spars. This additional length extending out is used to lash the cross spar to the stakes, which anchor the ends of the walkway in place.

After the first cross spar is lashed in place, add six more 3-foot cross spars every 16 to 18 inches down the length of the lateral spars. The last cross spar should be lashed about 12 inches from the ends of the lateral spars to allow room for the "underspar."

Underspar – An important feature of this type of walkway is to lash one 3-1/2-foot cross spar to the underside of the lateral spars 6 inches from the end. When the two walkway sections are

Lashing on the Walkway's Underspar

237

placed on the trestle(s) to form the bridge, these underspars should contact the transom of the trestle(s). Then the three spars [two underspars on the two walkways and the transom spar of the trestle(s)] are lashed together at three points using strop lashings.

On most bridges, walkways come from both directions to meet at the trestle(s). The connection between the walkway underspars and the transom spar is what makes these walkway

bridge designs so ingenious, and joining these subassemblies together in this fashion never ceases to capture the imagination of the Scouts building the bridge.

PROJECT BUILDING: Two Basic Subassemblies

Walkway plank – Before lashing the walkway to the trestle, the walkway plank should be lashed on in at least three places. A square lashing with a 20-foot lashing rope does the trick, or use strop lashings.

Strop Lashings – When a quick job is desired with light spars, a simple strop lashing will often suffice. Find the middle of the length of binder twine or lashing rope and then proceed to tightly wrap both ends simultaneously in opposite directions around the poles finishing with a Square Knot. A strop lashing is completed without taking any frapping turns.

Square Lashing the Walkway Plank with 1/4" Manila

If you choose to use strop lashings for the walkway planks, reach down and wrap the middle of the rope or binder twine under one of the cross spars. Then wrap the line over the walkway plank and down under the cross spar at the other side of the plank. Do this two or three times and finish with a Square Knot.

Anchoring the walkway – After the walkway is assembled, the butt ends are placed on the bank of the creek or ravine. This end is anchored in place by driving stakes in the outside corners formed by the lateral spars and the first (3-1/2-foot) cross spar. Lash this cross spar of the walkway to the stakes with a strop lashing.

Driving in Stakes in the Outside Corners to Anchor the Walkway

When the walkways are lashed to the stakes and to the trestle(s), all the walkway sections become joined to form a single unit that is very strong.

Shorter or longer walkways using 8 or 12-foot sections are just fine but, especially with longer spars, be sure to test their strength before lashing them into a walkway that could be unsafe.

PROJECT BUILDING: Two Basic Subassemblies

Two pre-tested, 10-foot walkways soundly support eleven Scouts on a Single A-Frame Bridge.

SCOUT PIONEERING — Ol' Fashioned Outdoor Fun!

- Single A-Frame Bridge -

In the pioneering village at the national jamboree, two side-by-side, Single A-Frame Bridges are poised, in the early morning.

"Building this bridge is quite simple because there are very few lashings needed for the center A-frame. The A-frame is a triangular shape that resists racking and provides strength for the structure." — Adolph Peschke

PROJECT BUILDING: Single A-Frame Bridge

Here's what you'll need:

- two 10 to 12-foot x 3-inch A-frame legs (depending on how deep the creek or ravine)
- one 6-foot x 2-inch bottom ledger
- one 6-foot x 3-inch transom
- four 10-foot x 3-inch walkway lateral spars
- twelve 3-foot x 2-inch walkway cross spars
- four 3-1/2-foot x 2-inch walkway cross spars
- two 10-foot x 10-inch x 2-inch walkway planks
- six pioneering stakes and two small sticks for 1-1 anchors
- two guylines

A-Frame – Start this project by determining the depth of the creek or ravine to be spanned. You have to add 8 feet to that measurement to get the total height of the legs for the A-frame. For example, to span a creek 4 feet deep, the legs of the A-frame should be about 12 feet or longer. This total length allows for the distance from the butt ends of the A-frame legs up to the transom that supports the walkways. The transom should be about 1 foot higher than the banks of the creek. It also allows for the height from the walkways up to the tops of the legs, to permit free passage for a person along the walkways. Lay the A-frame subassembly out on the ground to check if the spars are long enough when lashed together to meet these two height requirements.

Left: Shear Lashing at the Top / Right: Square Lashings for the Ledger & Transom

Walkways – The two 10-foot walkway sections are made as separate subassemblies. (See Walkways, page 234.)

A-frame Legs – When you've determined the length of the spars for the legs of the A-frame, lash them together at the top with a sturdy shear lashing.

Ledger and Transom – To complete the A-frame, use square lashings to lash the bottom ledger across the legs about 1 foot from the bottom of the legs. Then lash a transom spar to

PROJECT BUILDING: *Single A-Frame Bridge*

support the walkways at the proper height in relation to the banks of the creek.

Attach the Guylines. Using Roundturns with Two Half Hitches or Rolling Hitches, add a 1/4-inch guyline to the top of each leg, about 3/4 of the way up. These will prevent the A-frame from tipping over. On each bank, about 20 feet from where the A-frame will be positioned, drive a stake into the ground at a 20° angle.

Assembly – After the walkways and A-frame are made, take them to the assembly site. Place the A-frame in the center of the creek and heel in the legs about 4 to 6 inches deep. As the

Top: Transporting A-Frame /
Middle: Positioning A-Frame /
Bottom: Placing Walkways

legs are being heeled in, level the transom to accept the walkways in a level position.

When the A-frame is upright and the transom is level, lash both underspars on the walkways to the transom with strop lashings at three points. Next, lash the cross spars at the ends of the walkways to stakes on the banks of the creek with strop lashings. (A strop lashing is easy to tie. Halve the rope, place the midpoint behind what you're lashing, wrap both ends around the spars a few times and finish with a Square Knot.) As a final measure, attach the guylines to the stakes, driven into the ground 20 feet away on either side, with rope tackles.

PROJECT BUILDING

- Single Trestle Bridge -

This simple crossing bridge uses only a single trestle and two walkways. The legs of the trestle are extended up above the walkways to provide a way to attach handrails. This project can be broken into four subassemblies: the trestle, the two walkways, and the handrails. The length of the spars listed for the walkways and trestle will be enough to build a bridge that will span a creek or ravine that's up to 4 feet deep and 18 feet wide.

Here's what you'll need:

- two 8 or 10-foot x 3-inch trestle legs
- one 4-foot x 3-inch trestle transom
- one 4-foot x 2-inch trestle ledger
- two 6-foot x 2-inch cross braces
- four 10-foot x 3-inch walkway lateral spars
- twelve 3-foot x 2-inch walkway cross spars
- four 3-1/2-foot x 2-inch walkway cross spars
- two 10-foot x 10-inch x 2-inch walkway planks
- four 12-foot x 2-1/2-inch handrails
- four pioneering stakes

Trestle – The legs for the trestle should be spars that are about 3 inches in diameter and 8 to 10 feet long. When choosing these spars, take into account the depth of the creek you're crossing. The distance from the base of the legs to the top ledger (transom) on the trestle should be about 1 foot higher than the level of the banks of the creek. This will allow the walkways to slant up. Then allow an additional 4 feet in height on the legs from the top ledger up to the top of the legs for attaching the handrails.

PROJECT BUILDING: Single Trestle Bridge

The top ledger of the trestle should be about 3 inches in diameter since it also acts as the transom and carries all the weight of the walkways and the person using it. The bottom ledger can be smaller—a 2-inch diameter spar will work here.

Walkways – The two walkways are assembled as separate subassemblies. *Make sure the 3-1/2-foot cross spars at the ends of the walkway extend far enough out to attach both the stakes and the handrails without interfering with the passageway.* (See Walkways, page 234.)

Left: Positioning the Trestle / Right: Lashing the Underspars to the Transom

Lashing the Handrails to the Trestle Legs

Assembly – To assemble the bridge, set the trestle in the center of the creek. Heel in the bottoms of the trestle legs by setting them in holes approximately 4 to 6 inches deep. This will prevent the trestle from shifting, and is also a way to level the transom spar as the trestle is set in place so the walkways are level.

Next, put the walkways in position from both sides and lash the walkways' underspars to the transom (top ledger) of the trestle in three places using strop lashings. (A strop lashing

PROJECT BUILDING: Single Trestle Bridge

is easy to tie. Halve the rope, place the midpoint behind what you're lashing, wrap both ends around the spars a few times and finish with a Square Knot.)

Once the underspars of the walkways are lashed to the transom, and the walkways are extending out onto the sides of the stream or ravine, it's time to anchor the ends. To accomplish this, drive stakes at the other end of the walkways and lash the 3-1/2-foot cross spars to them.

Left: Driving in the Pioneering Stakes / Right: Lashing the Walkways to the Stakes

Handrails – One of the Single Trestle Bridge's outstanding features are the handrails. They're not only provided to help those crossing the bridge, but also add strength to the overall structure. When the handrails are added, they form triangles with the walkway and the trestle leg which prevent the bridge from racking. Lash the handrails to the top of the trestle legs with square lashings and to the stakes with simple strop lashings.

Pioneering Merit Badge Class Posing on their Single Trestle Bridge

PROJECT BUILDING

- Single Lock Bridge -

This is a well-established design for a Scout Pioneering bridge. Over the years it has stood out as a remarkable example of real Scout engineering and many past BSA publications featured photos of Scouts lashing the walkways to the trestles while constructing the bridge over a stream.

The spars included in the following list of materials will build a bridge to span a creek or ravine approximately 4 feet deep and 18 feet from bank to bank:

253

- four 6-foot x 3-inch trestle legs
- four 4-foot x 2-1/2-inch trestle ledgers
- one 4-foot x 3-inch trestle transom spar
- four 6-foot x 2-inch cross braces
- four 10-foot x 3-inch walkway lateral spars
- twelve 3-foot x 2-inch walkway cross spars
- four 3-1/2-foot x 2-inch walkway cross spars
- two 10-foot x 10-inch x 2-inch walkway planks
- four pioneering stakes

The bridge consists of four distinct subassemblies: two trestles and two walkways.

Trestles – If necessary, adjust the length of the spars for the trestle so that when they are placed in the creek, the tops of the ledgers will be about 1 foot above the level of the bank. This will give a comfortable slant to the walkways. Here are two points to remember when preparing the trestles:

1. When lashing on the top ledgers, leave enough space from the top so when the legs interlock, there's enough room to fit the transom.
2. When constructing the two trestles, build only one trestle first. Then as the second trestle is being built, make sure

PROJECT BUILDING: Single Lock Bridge

the legs are narrower at the top and fit between the legs of the first trestle.

The legs of one trestle must fit between the legs of the other.

Transporting the Trestles to a Ravine

Walkways – Here's a quick walkway recap: Each walkway consists of two lateral spars, six cross spars, and two longer cross spars. One of these two longer cross spars is used as an underspar at the end of the walkway that is attached to the transom. The other longer cross spar is used to anchor the walkways to the stakes. (See Walkways, page 234.)

Assembly – After building the trestles and walkways, take them to the assembly site (the creek or ravine). Place the

PROJECT BUILDING: Single Lock Bridge

trestles in the center of the creek so that the tops of the trestles are interlocked. Then lift the 3-inch diameter transom spar to fit on top of the interlocked trestle legs.

Left: Trestles Interlocked / Right: Transom Spar Positioned on Top

Now, heel in the bases of the legs in holes 4 to 6 inches deep. As you're heeling in the legs, level the transom spar so the walkways don't slant when they're added.

Next, the two walkways are put into position. Lash the underspars on the walkways to the transom spar with strop lashings at three points. (A strop lashing is easy to tie. Halve the rope, place the midpoint behind what you're lashing, wrap both ends around the spars a few times and finish with a Square Knot.)

Anchoring the Walkways – Finally, to anchor the walkways, drive the stakes in the outside corners formed by the lateral walkway spars and the first (3-1/2-foot) cross spars, and lash the ends of the walkways to the stakes. By lashing the walkways to the transom spar and lashing the ends of the walkways to the stakes, you make a complete walkway unit that will prevent movement and provide a sturdy bridge deck.

Scouts make some final adjustments to their Single Lock Bridge (photo scanned from the Boy Scout *Fieldbook*, 2nd Edition).

PROJECT BUILDING

- Camp Seesaw -

The Camp Seesaw is one of many pioneering, playground structures. Requiring less time, materials, and expertise than the Camp Swing and Swing Boat, it's one of the easiest to assemble.

The project was inspired by *Fun With Ropes and Spars* by John Thurman who, with his inimitable approach to providing pioneering challenges and robust Scouting activities,

John Thurman's Underwater Seesaw

playfully dubbed it the "Underwater Seesaw."

This version is a readily-doable land approach that can be constructed during a camping trip (where the materials are trailered in) or along side a Double A-frame Monkey Bridge as part of an impressive, public demonstration of Scouting fun at a Scout Expo. What we've got here is a large, campsite toy that's relatively easy to build.

Here's a list of the basic materials:

- four 8 to 10-foot x 4-inch leg spars
- two 6-foot x 3-inch leg supports
- two 2 to 3-foot x 3-inch roller supports
- three 2 to 3-foot x 2-inch connectors
- one six-foot x 4-1/2-inch roller spar
- one 10-foot x 8-inch x 2-inch smooth plank
- twelve 15-foot x 1/4-inch lashing ropes
- four 20-foot x 1/4-inch lashing ropes for the roller supports

PROJECT BUILDING: Camp Seesaw

- one 35-foot x 1/4-inch lashing rope for the plank
- four 25-foot x 3/8-inch guylines
- two old tires
- eight 30-inch pioneering stakes

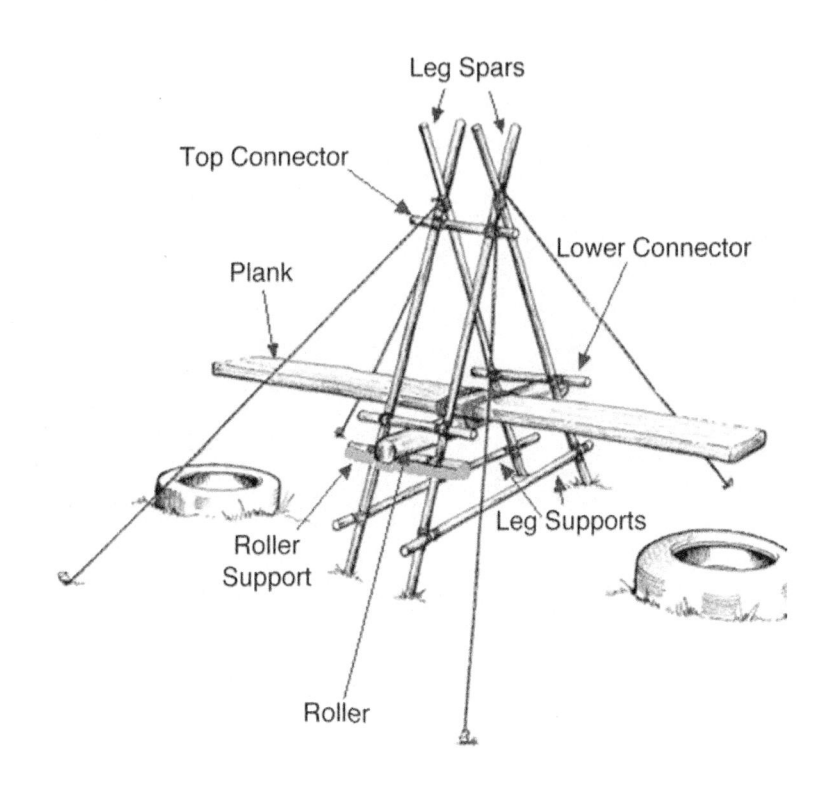

SCOUT PIONEERING — Ol' Fashioned Outdoor Fun!

Camp Seesaw as a Festival Exhibit

Though this is a simple project, some precision will be required when positioning the plank at the right height so that riders don't experience too much tilt.

PROJECT BUILDING: Camp Seesaw

In building the seesaw, the premise is to space the A-frames, the roller supports and the two lower connectors so that the 6-foot roller spar can easily roll around, but can just barely move from side to side or up and down.

Like with any seesaw, care must be taken not to misuse the structure. Overall, this camp seesaw is a tempting attraction and gets a lot of long-time play and attention. When built with care and guyed down securely, it can withstand the frequent use it invariably will get, even from heavier riders. (See the advisories at the end of this section.)

Build the A-frames. The first step is to prepare two *matching* A-frames using the leg spars and the 6-foot leg support spars. You can use a shear lashing or a square lashing on top, and square lashings for the 6-foot leg support spars. The main thing is to make sure that with both A-frames, the tops intersect the same distance from the tips and the legs spread apart an equal distance at the butt ends. The 6-foot leg supports can be lashed on 8 inches up from the bottom and protrude 8 inches out from each side. The tips of the legs can intersect a foot from the top.

SCOUT PIONEERING — Ol' Fashioned Outdoor Fun!

Prepare to connect the A-frames. Stand the A-frames up so that the legs and support spars are parallel, about 4-1/2 inches apart. Since the roller spar will eventually be rotating between the A-frames, the actual distance the A-frames are apart is determined by the diameter of the roller spar. Four Scouts should hold the A-frames upright and steady.

Lash on the roller support spars. Measure about 30 inches up from the butt ends of all four legs. *(For smaller, shorter riders, it's advisable to make this height lower.)* The height of the roller support spars will determine the angle of the board. Too steep an angle could easily make riding precarious. Begin connecting the two A-frames by lashing on the roller supports with *tight* square lashings. Lash them to the outside of the legs at a distance just

Tightly Lashing on a Roller Support

PROJECT BUILDING: Camp Seesaw

a fraction wider than the diameter of the roller spar. For neatness, space them so the ends extend an equal distance out from the A-frame legs. Because these roller supports will be bearing the weight of the heavy roller spar, the plank, and the Scouts playing on the seesaw, when lashing them on with a Mark II Square Lashing, start the lashing by tying a Constrictor Knot around the leg to minimize any slippage.

Lash on the lower connectors. With the A-frames held steadily upright, temporarily lay the 6-foot roller spar on top of the supports. Using the diameter of the 6-foot roller spar as a measure, continue to connect the two A-frames by lashing on the two lower connectors at a distance just above the roller spar, with tight square lashings. Again, for neatness, space them so the ends extend an equal distance out from the A-frame legs. Remove the roller and set it aside.

Lashing on the Top Connector

265

Lash on the top connector. Lash the last connector to one of the legs at the top of each A-frame, just below where the legs cross. If there's difficulty reaching the point on the legs where this connector needs to be lashed, carefully lay both parallel A-frames on their sides and then lash the connector in place. Again, for neatness, space the connector so the ends extend an equal distance out from the A-frame legs.

Make the Anchors. Build four 1-1 Anchors 45° out from each leg.

Attach the guylines. Using Rolling Hitches, or Roundturns with Two Half Hitches, tie on the four guylines, each about two feet below the square lashings at the top of the A-frames.

Position the seesaw. Stand up and move the A-frames in the position you want the seesaw. Drive in each of the four pioneering stakes, fifteen feet away and 45° out from where they're tied to the legs of the A-frames. Then, connect a guyline to each using a Roundturn with Two Half Hitches or rope tackle.

Lash on the plank. Slide the roller spar on top of the roller supports. Lay the plank on top of the roller and using the

35-foot lashing rope, lash the middle of the plank firmly in place with a square lashing. It's desirable to equip the plank with some spaced handholds. (See the advisories, below.)

Lay down the tires. On each side, at the point where the plank hits the ground, place a tire to cushion the impact and absorb the shock.

CAMP SEESAW ADVISORIES

- Seesaws can be hazardous. Make sure there's no horseplay—just seated cooperation.
- When riders take their places on the board, they should position themselves so their weight is balanced.
- Riders should never kick off from the ground forcefully springing their side skyward which can easily unbalance the other rider.
- Exiting the seesaw should only be done when both rider's feet are on the ground.
- Adding ropes for handholds can be done in various places along the board by drilling holes about two inches from each edge and threading a short length of 3/8" to 1/2" braided nylon or polyester, and tying a couple of figure eight stopper

knots or tying the ends together on the underside of the board with a water knot http://programresources.org/water-knot.

- Making four indentation grooves in the plank where the wraps of the square lashing will lie when it's lashed to the roller bar will eliminate the plank slipping towards one or the other rider during use.

Camp Seesaw Built and Manned by a Scout Troop during a Webeloree

PROJECT BUILDING

- Camp Swing -

Though it does present some interesting challenges, the design for this swing is not complicated. A well-working swing is going to get lots of play. Therefore, lashings need to be super tight, and the eight sturdy pioneering stakes that serve as anchors need to be driven solidly into the ground, perpendicular to and touching the six spars connecting the legs. The building crew for this project should include some older, stronger Scouts.

Here are the materials:

- six 12-foot x 3-1/2-inch spars for the legs
- one 12-foot x 4-inch spar for the crossbar
- six 6-foot x 3-inch connecting spars
- eight long pioneering stakes
- two 2-foot x 2-inch x 8-inch prepared swing seats
- four 20-foot x 1/2-inch swing ropes
- four steel rings
- four 6-foot x 5/8-inch ropes for Prusiks
- twenty 15-foot x 1/4-inch manila lashing ropes
- six 20-foot x 1/4-inch manila lashing ropes
- two single pulleys reeved with 20 feet of rope, with a small loop of rope tied to the top
- one eight-foot ladder

Though one might think this structure is built by making two simple tripods to support the crossbar, it's *better* to make two A-frames, standing up vertically, supported by a third spar lashed to one leg of each A-frame, slanting down to the ground. The obvious reason is to give the crossbar maximum stability

PROJECT BUILDING: Camp Swing

where it rests at the juncture of the two legs of each vertical A-frame.

Prepare the A-Frames. Using two 12-foot spars and one 6-foot spar, with tight square lashings, lash together two identical A-frames making sure the tips of the legs cross the same distance from the top for each. Use a 20-foot rope where the tips of the legs intersect, and 15-foot ropes at the bottom.

Make sure the 6-foot connecting spars are lashed low enough to the bottom so later on there will be plenty of room to lash them to the pioneering stakes.

Add the oblique supporting legs. About a foot or so below the top lashing on the A-frames, lash on a third 12-foot spar to one leg of each A-frame, using 20-foot ropes. These spars will be angled down, extending out to support the A-frames in their vertical positions.

Connect the legs. Stand up the A-frames so they're in a vertical position. Connect the 12-foot oblique supporting leg to the legs of each A-frame, using the remaining 6-foot spars and eight 15-foot ropes. Again, make sure they're lashed low enough to the ground so later on there will be plenty of room to lash them to the pioneering stakes. (If you'll be using the pulleys to lift up the 12-foot crossbar, loop one over the top of a leg on each side, before standing up the A-frames.)

Position the two 3-legged subassemblies. Line up both support assemblies so they are facing one another on even ground and with the A-frames 10 feet apart.

Prepared Swing Seats

Rig the swing seats. Attach two 20 foot swing ropes to the two swing seats, using a Scaffold Hitch rigged with a Bowline. In order to accommodate the swing rope with the Scaffold Hitch, the swing seats should be prepared with

PROJECT BUILDING: Camp Swing

impressions cut on each side, 2 inches long and 1/2 inch deep, beginning 1-1/2 inches from each end.

Attach the rings to the crossbar. Using the 6-foot ropes, tie the steel rings to the crossbar with Prusiks at intervals as per the measurements reflected in the diagram.

Spacing Along the Crossbar

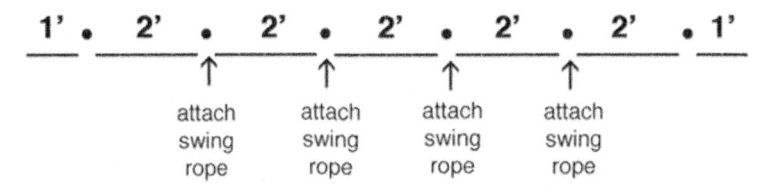

1' . 2' . 2' . 2' . 2' . 2' . 1'

↑ attach swing rope   ↑ attach swing rope   ↑ attach swing rope   ↑ attach swing rope

Position the crossbar. Tie one end of each pulley rope to the ends of the crossbar, and have two Scouts carefully hoist the crossbar up to near the tops of the A-frames. They must carefully hold it in place. Position the ladder so that it's even with one A-frame, so a strong, older Scout can climb about four to five feet up and lift the end into the crux of one A-frame. This process is then repeated on the other side of the swing.

Lash on the crossbar. Making sure the rings are properly hanging down, and the crossbar is extending out approximately 1 foot from each side, one Scout will climb up and *tightly* lash the crossbar to one of the legs of each A-frame.

Tie on the swings. One Scout will climb up and connect the swing ropes to the rings using a Roundturn with Two Half Hitches, making sure the swings hang evenly at the desired height.

Lashing Pioneering Stakes to a Ledger as Anchors

Drive in and lash on the anchors. Four pioneering stakes are driven into the ground on each side—two spaced evenly and touching the bottom of each A-frame, and one against each connecting spar, hammered in near the oblique

PROJECT BUILDING: *Camp Swing*

supporting leg. After these stakes are solidly in the ground, so they cannot jiggle, tightly lash them to the connecting spars using 15-foot ropes.

Test the swing. As two Scouts sit on the seats and swing, a couple of Scouts observe how everything remains stable. Before making the swing available for use by other Scouts, make any necessary adjustments.

View "Scout Swing" https://youtu.be/cqkV_JVbyyY

- Swing Boat -

Two Scouts acquaint themselves with how to have fun on a swing boat, in the pioneering area at the national jamboree. Riders swing by grabbing the pull rope attached to the opposite side from where they are seated.

A swing boat is a fairground ride on which pairs of riders pull ropes to swing back and forth. This is a smaller, Scout-sized version, but still lots of fun and plenty big enough. There are certain logistical challenges associated with this project, but nothing unmanageable. As when building the camp swing, an 8-foot or taller folding ladder will be very useful. A good, able-bodied crew is necessary.

PROJECT BUILDING: Swing Boat

Here's what you'll need:

- six 12-foot x 4-inch spars
- six 10-foot x 4-inch spars
- two 6-foot x 3-inch spars
- eighteen 20-foot x 1/4-inch lashing ropes
- two 36-foot x 1/2-inch swing ropes
- four 36-foot x 3/8-inch guylines
- twelve pioneering stakes
- one 8-foot x 8-inch x 2-inch prepared plank (sanded and notched about 6 inches from the ends)
- two rope grommets with steel rings (optional)

Build the A-frames. Using 20-foot ropes, lash together two identical A-frames. The top lashing should be approximately 3 feet below the tips of the 12-foot legs. (In lieu of shear lashings you might want to join the legs at the top with moderately tight square lashings applied with the legs held at 90°, after which the legs can be brought into the desired position to add the ledgers. But in doing so, make sure there won't be too much strain applied to the top rope and the spars.) The 10-foot ledgers need to be approximately 1 foot above the butts of the legs. For added stability, on each A-frame, lash on a 6-foot crossbar.

PROJECT BUILDING: Swing Boat

After they're built, the A-frames are stood up and held in place, while other construction continues.

Join the A-frames together. Stand up the A-frames and holding them in place, use the remaining 12-foot spars to join them together. Lash these on as low as possible so they don't interfere with the action of the swing.

The following steps can be carried out using an 8 to 10-foot folding step ladder or by laying the structure on its side. Either way, strong crew members will be needed to hold the spars in place.

Tightening a Square Lashing on One of the Parallel Top Support Spars

PROJECT BUILDING: Swing Boat

Add the Center Spar. With *tight* square lashings, about one foot from each end, lash a stout 10-foot center spar to the inside of one leg of each A-frame where the tops intersect. This will provide a good, inward lean to the A-frames. (If you're using rope grommets with steel rings, attach them to the center spar with a Prusik.)

Lash on the parallel top support spars. Join the tops of the A frames by tightly lashing a 10-foot spar on the legs of each A-frame, about 6 inches from the tips. (It's a good idea to start these lashings with a Constrictor Knot to minimize slippage during use.)

Attach the pull rope spar and pull ropes. At right angles, lash a 10-foot spar across the center for the pull ropes. About 6 inches from the ends, tightly tie a 15-foot pull rope to each end with a Roundturn with Two Half Hitches.

Attach the swing. Attach a swing rope to each end of the prepared plank with a Scaffold Hitch. Using a Roundturn with Two Half Hitches, tie the ends of each swing rope securely to their corresponding ring -or- directly to the center spar.

Add the guylines. Using a Roundturn with Two Half Hitches or Rolling Hitch, attach a 36-foot x 3/8-inch guyline to the top of each leg. (If, the structure has been on its side, it's time to stand it completely up.)

Lashing the Bottom Ledger to the Pioneering Stake Anchors

Prepare the anchors. Drive in pioneering stakes for four 1-1 anchors extending 20 feet out from the legs at 45°. Attach the corresponding guyline to each using a rope tackle. Also, solidly drive in an intersecting stake against the A-frame ledgers about 6 inches from each of the four corners. Tightly lash each stake to the corresponding ledger with a square lashing.

PROJECT BUILDING: Swing Boat

Make adjustments. Level out the plank to the desired height and adjust the swing ropes so the swing hangs evenly.

Scouts enjoy the swing boat built for an Order of the Arrow conclave.

View "Scout Pioneering: Small Swing Boat" https://youtu.be/vdNeLePndcg

SCOUT PIONEERING — Ol' Fashioned Outdoor Fun!

- Four Flag Gateway Tower -

This majestic project, fashioned along the lines of Adolph's 14' Double Ladder Signal Tower, is an impressive feat of Scout engineering.

While in actuality it's a tower that requires hoisting, it's also a tall gateway, and quite an elaborate flag display. When flags are lashed to each corner and the wind blows, the effect this project creates is spectacular.

PROJECT BUILDING: Four Flag Gateway Tower

Here are the materials you'll need:

- four 14-foot x 2-1/2-inch leg spars
- six 8-foot x 2-inch X-brace spars
- four 6-foot x 2-inch X-brace spars
- four 6-foot x 2-inch support spars
- six 4-foot x 2-inch leg spreaders
- forty-five 15-foot x 1/4-inch lashing ropes
- eight 6 to 10-foot x 1/4-inch lashing ropes (for flags)
- four 35-foot x 3/8-inch guylines
- eight 24-inch pioneering stakes

This project consists of several sub-assemblies. With an intelligent division of labor, it can be built in good order e.g. building both of the Four-Foot-Sides while simultaneously, laying out the position of the legs and building the anchors.

Assemble the Four-Foot-Sides. Begin by laying out two pairs of 14-foot spars for the tower legs, side by side, each about 3-1/2 feet apart. Be sure the butt ends are even at the bottom so the tower will stand up straight. With square lashings, lash each pair of legs together starting with a 4-foot bottom leg spreader about 6 inches up from the butt ends. Then,

SCOUT PIONEERING — Ol' Fashioned Outdoor Fun!

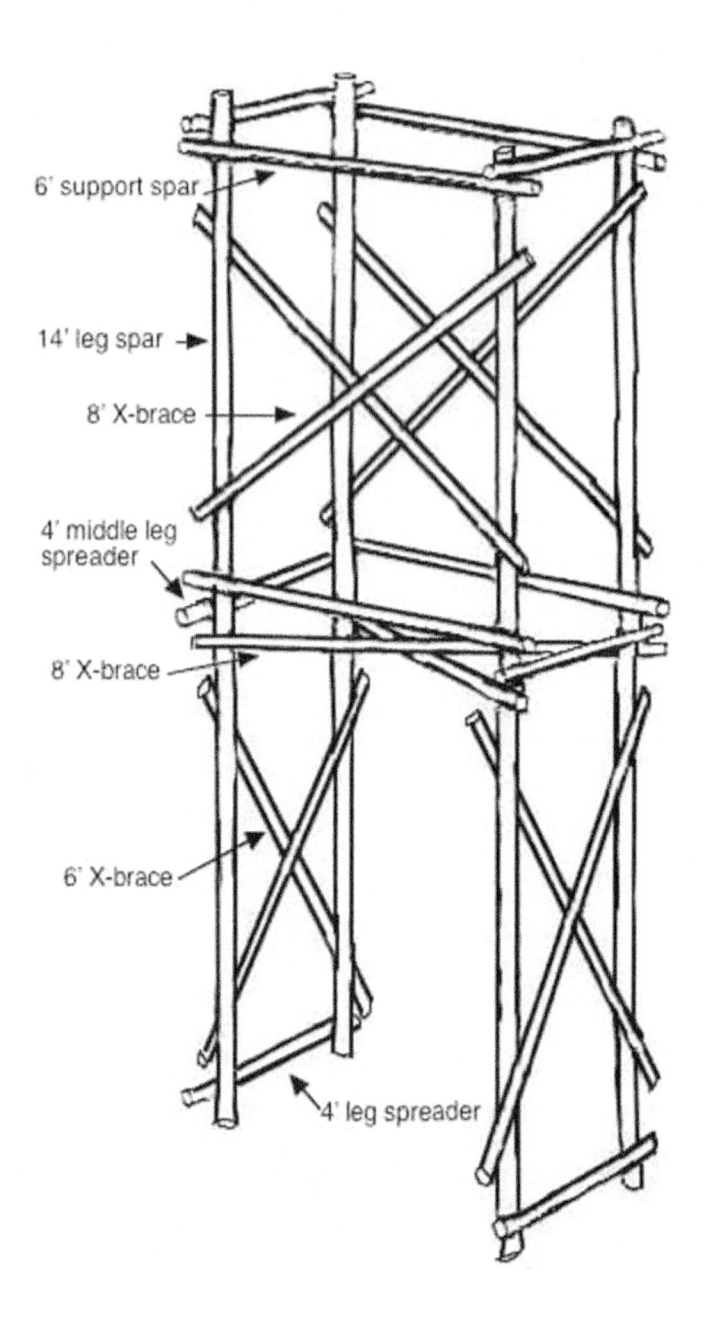

- 6' support spar
- 14' leg spar
- 8' X-brace
- 4' middle leg spreader
- 8' X-brace
- 6' X-brace
- 4' leg spreader

PROJECT BUILDING: *Four Flag Gateway Tower*

lash on one of the 4-foot leg spreaders in the middle of the 14-foot legs (7 feet up), and a 4-foot top spreader about 3 inches from the top of the 14-foot legs.

When the legs of each Four-Foot-Side are joined with the three 4-foot spreaders, lash on two 6-foot X-braces using square lashings, to join the ends to the legs, and a diagonal or Mark II Square lashing where they cross, forming a trestle in the bottom half of the legs. (Remember, three of the ends are lashed to one side of the legs, and one on the other side, so that a slight gap is created where they cross. Spring them together with either of these lashings.)

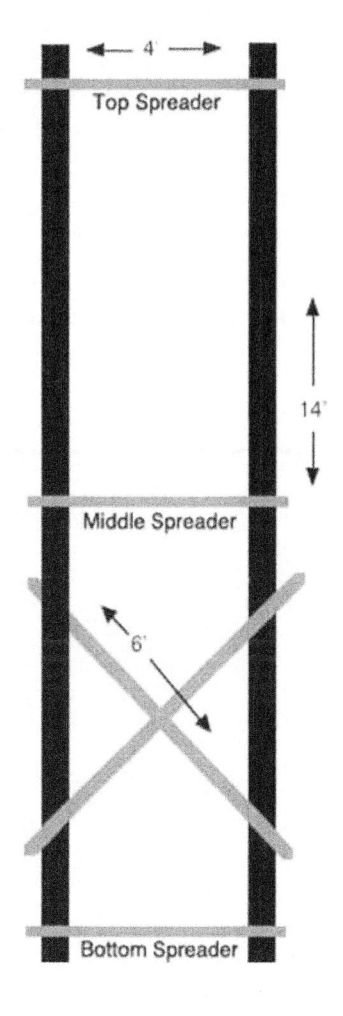

Joining Together One of the Four-Foot-Sides – Turn both sides up horizontally, parallel to one another about 5-1/2

287

feet apart. Make sure the bottoms are even. Lash on one of the 6-foot support spars directly above the 4-foot middle spreader. Lash another one of the 6-foot support spars directly under the 4-foot side spreader at the very top.

The next thing to do is to lash on two of the 8-foot X-brace spars diagonally between the two 6-foot supports using square lashings to join the ends to the legs, and a diagonal lashing or Mark II Square Lashing where they cross, forming a trestle in the top part of the wide (6-foot) side.

Join the other side. To make the lashings to join the other side, you have to get the whole crew together to carefully lift and roll the tower over 180° so that it's laying on the X-brace, making it much easier to lash together the other side.

PROJECT BUILDING: Four Flag Gateway Tower

Carefully Lifting and Rolling to Join the Remaining Sides

Lashing on the Middle X-Brace – This X-brace is what will keep the sides from racking. Lash the two remaining 8-foot X-brace spars diagonally across the legs just under the 4-foot middle leg spreader. Use square lashings to lash them to the legs and a diagonal lashing or the Mark II Square Lashing where they cross. To accomplish this, some crew members will have to hold up the top of the tower so there will be better access to all four ends of the 8-foot X-brace spars.

Lashing on the Flags – Lash the flagpoles of the four selected flags to the top of each tower leg using a couple of tight round lashings.

Anchors and Guylines – When all the lashings are done, move the tower to where it will be hoisted. This design is not

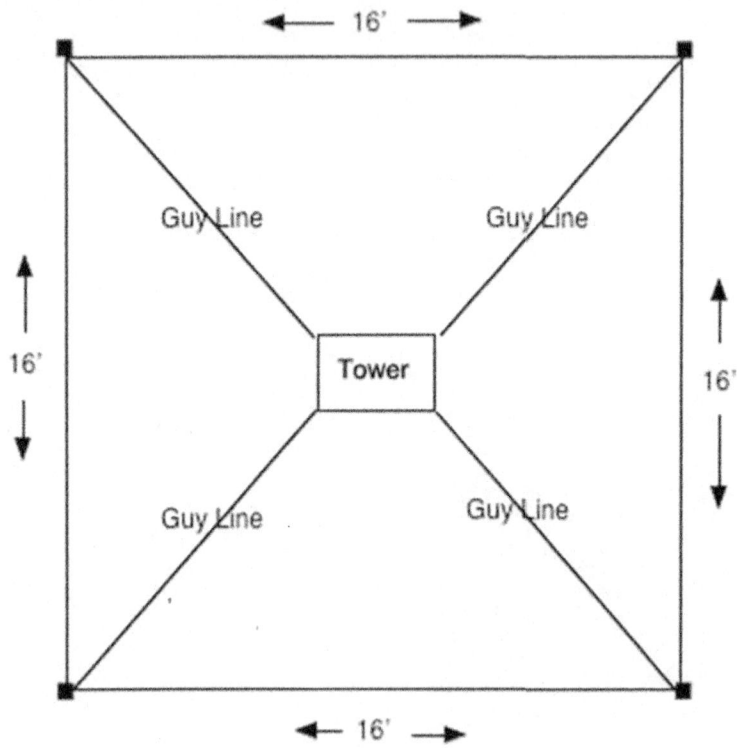

freestanding. Therefore, allowing for the necessary guylines, it requires a space wide and deep enough to accommodate a 16-foot x 16-foot area. Lay out the position of the four legs on the

PROJECT BUILDING: Four Flag Gateway Tower

ground. Then determine where the four anchors for the guylines will be placed to steady the legs of the tower. Using the pioneering stakes, build four 1-1 anchors. Each should extend 16 feet, and 45° out from the legs.

Before Hoisting the Tower – Attach the four guylines securely to the legs, about 10 feet up, with Rolling Hitches or Roundturns with Two Half Hitches. *Before hoisting the tower, double check to see all the flagpoles are lashed securely, and make sure the flags are neatly unfurled.*

Hoisting the Tower – You'll need a whole crew to do the hoisting. Get ready to hoist the tower by delegating the following:

- One signal caller who tells the crew members when and how hard to pull on the ropes
- One safety officer who's on the look out for all safety considerations and signs of trouble during the hoisting
- Four Scouts to serve as "lifters," to lift the top 6-foot support spar that's on the ground, whose job it is to first lift and then push the tower up

- Two Scouts, one on each of the two guylines attached to the legs of the 6-foot side that's on the ground, to make sure the tower isn't over pulled and topples over
- Four "pullers" who will use the two guylines facing up as hoisting ropes to pull the tower until it's standing

When everyone is in position, the signal caller should direct the Scouts on the hoisting ropes (the pullers) to hoist the tower into position, while the lifters start lifting. Care should be exercised not to over pull the tower. As soon as the tower is standing, four Scouts should temporarily tie the guylines to the anchors using a Roundturn with Two Half Hitches. Later, a rope tackle will be configured for each guyline.

Heeling the Tower – If the tower is uneven, the butt ends of the legs can be heeled in as deep as needed, to make it more level.

Tightening the Guylines – As soon as the tower is in position, go to each of the anchors and untie the Roundturn with Two Half Hitches and replace it with a rope tackle. Use the rope tackles to hold the tower steady, by gradually applying strain to each of the four guylines at the same time. Do this by tying a Butterfly Knot in each guyline about 6 to 8 feet from

PROJECT BUILDING: Four Flag Gateway Tower

A Four Flag Gateway Tower with halyards applied to 20-foot leg spars is built at the entrance to the Scoutcraft area at the James C. Justice National Scout Camp.

the anchor. Then wrap the running end of the guyline around the forward stake of the anchor and back through the loop in the Butterfly Knot (refer to rope tackle). When rope tackles are tied to each of the four anchors, gradually tighten the lines. Apply enough strain to each of the guylines to hold the tower firm and in a vertical position. Then tie off the rope tackles by securing the running ends with half hitches.

Hoisting a tower in itself is an exhilarating experience, and even more so when the tower is flying your flags!

SCOUT PIONEERING — Ol' Fashioned Outdoor Fun!

These Scouts are elated after building their Four Flag Gateway Tower at the main entrance of the Scout Expo for their council.

PROJECT BUILDING

14' Double Ladder Tower -

This book wouldn't be complete without including one of our all-time favorite pioneering projects. After experiencing success with the Double A-Frame Monkey Bridge, all the necessary materials were procured to construct Adolph's Scout-sized, 14' Double Ladder Signal Tower. The first time we built it was during a camping trip in proximity to a Native American Powwow. Four of our troop's junior leaders spent hours bonding together upon the platform, well after dark. A couple of months later, we proudly put one up as our troop's exhibit during a council Scout Expo.

Troop Tower Display, 1997 District Scout Expo

Since those days, the BSA had imposed certain height restrictions relating to pioneering projects designed for climbing. These restrictions were later adjusted so that with the proper review of the project by the Council Enterprise Risk Management Committee, in conjunction with the sound assurance the construction process will be carried out correctly and in accordance with pioneering safety guidelines, a structure like this that is taller than six feet can once again be built and climbed upon during Boy Scout summer camp.

As Adolph says, "The double ladder tower requires four 14-foot spars and several smaller spars, but not nearly the amount needed for a four-leg signal tower. It also cuts down the number of lashings required."

Adolph's design is not freestanding. Four guylines are employed to keep it upright and secure. What follows is a setup procedure along with some of his original diagrams:

Here are the required materials:

- four 14-foot x 4-inch tower legs
- ten 3-foot x 2-inch climbing ladder rungs
- three 3-foot x 2-inch support ladder spreaders
- two 6-foot x 2-1/2-inch base spreaders

PROJECT BUILDING: 14' Double Ladder Signal Tower

- two 6-foot x 2-1/2-inch platform supporting spars
- two 3-foot x 2-inch platform handrails
- two 6-foot x 2-inch platform long handrails
- four 10-foot x 2-1/2-inch X-braces
- two 8-foot x 2-1/2-inch X-braces
- eighteen 3-1/2 to 4-foot x 2-inch floor spars
- eight pioneering stakes
- four 50-foot x 3/8-inch manila guylines
- two 50-foot x 1/4 manila lashing ropes for floor lashings
- thirty-one 15-foot x 1/4-inch manila lashing ropes
- twenty-two 20-foot x 1/4-inch manila lashing ropes

Assemble the ladders. This project begins with building two ladders: a climbing ladder and a supporting ladder. Lay out two pairs of spars on the ground for the legs of the ladders. Be sure the butt ends are even at the bottom so the tower will stand

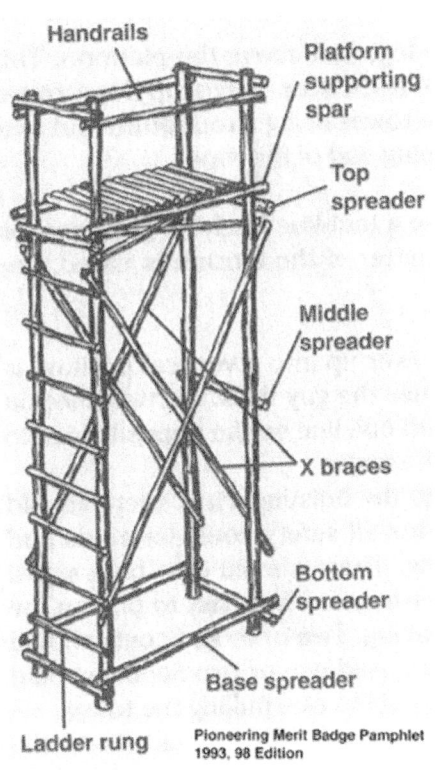

Scouts work together assembling the climbing ladder of their 14' Double Ladder Signal Tower.

up straight. Before you begin any lashing, mark the positions where the spars that will hold the top platform are to be lashed onto the legs. This will be about 4 feet from the top ends of the legs.

In order to make the climbing ladder, lash ten rungs on one pair of legs at about 1-foot intervals. The top rung should be lashed on where you marked the position of the platform, 4 feet from the top. Also the top handrail is lashed on to complete the climbing ladder.

To make the supporting ladder, lash three spars on the other set of legs to serve as the bottom, center, and top spreaders. The top spreader should be lashed at the point you marked for the platform, 4 feet from the top. Then lash on the top handrail, as on the climbing ladder.

PROJECT BUILDING: 14' Double Ladder Signal Tower

Lash the ladders together. Now you have to join the two ladders to form the tower. Turn the two ladders up on their sides so they're parallel to each other and approximately 6 feet apart. Check to see that the bottoms are even, then lash on the base spreader to join the bottoms of the two ladders.

Lash on the platform supporting spar just above the top rung and top spreader on the ladders. Before proceeding, check the measurements from the bottoms of the legs all the way to the platform supporting spar to make sure they're equal on both legs so that the platform will be level.

Continue by lashing on the top long handrail. Then lash on the two 10-foot side X-braces between the legs using square lashings to lash the ends to the legs, and a diagonal lashing (or Mark II Square Lashing) where they cross.

Rolling the Tower Over in Order to Lash the Other Side

299

Lash the other side. To make the lashings on the other side, the whole crew has to get together to roll the tower over 180° so that it's laying on the X braces. Repeat the same lashing process as for the previous side.

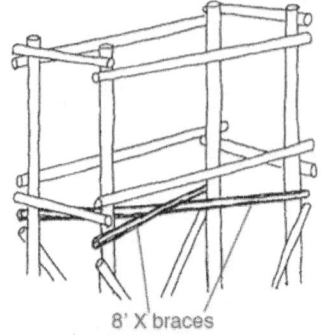

Lash on the 8-foot X braces. These important spars are lashed underneath the platform. In order to make these lashings on the bottom side, it will help if some crew members lift the legs.

8' X braces

Lash on the floor spars. Before standing the tower upright, with two tight floor lashings, lash on the spars to form the platform floor. Because the tower is on its side, it will be necessary for Scouts to hold the floor spars in place to keep them from sliding while the lashing is being completed.

Anchors and Guylines - When all the lashings are done, move the tower to where it will

PROJECT BUILDING: 14' Double Ladder Signal Tower

be hoisted. Before actually hoisting the tower, lay out the position of the four legs on the ground. After that, you can determine where the four anchors for the guylines will be placed to steady the legs of the tower.

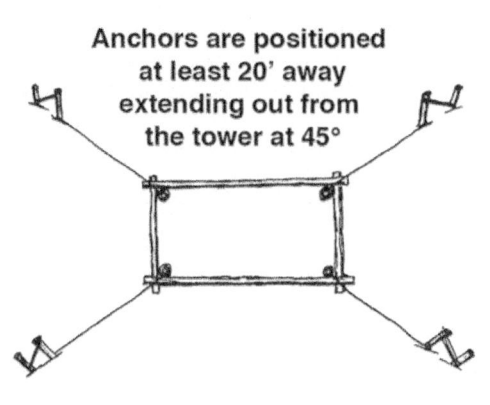

Anchors are positioned at least 20' away extending out from the tower at 45°

If the tower is positioned to make use of a natural anchor (such as a tree), prepare anchor strops to attach the guylines. For any guylines that won't be using natural anchors, build anchors using pioneering stakes. At a minimum, you'll need to build well constructed 1-1 anchors at all four corners.

Attach the four guylines to the legs just above the platform. The guylines should be 3/8-inch diameter manila or polypropylene rope. They're attached to the legs of the tower using a Roundturn with Two Half Hitches. Secure the running end of the rope.

Hoisting the tower - Hoisting the tower up into a vertical position can be an exhilarating experience. You'll need a whole crew to do the hoisting. First there should be a safety officer who observes for all safety considerations and signs of trouble during the hoisting. There should also be a signal caller who tells the crew members when and how fast to pull on the hoisting ropes and when to stop pulling. It's best to have at least two Scouts on each of the four guylines. The two front lines are for those Scouts doing the pulling, and the back lines

PROJECT BUILDING: 14' Double Ladder Signal Tower

to keep the tower from over pulling. The rest of the crew should help the pullers get the ball rolling by providing an initial lift.

When everyone is in position, the signal caller should direct the Scouts on the hoisting ropes to hoist the tower into position. As soon as it's up, temporarily tie the guylines to the anchors using a roundturn with two half hitches.

Heeling in the legs - When the tower is upright, heel in the butt ends of the tower legs in holes about 4 to 6 inches deep. This is done to steady the tower and can also help in evening out the tower to make sure the platform is level and the tower itself is vertical.

Tighten the guylines. To hold the tower steady, gradually apply strain to each of the four guylines at the same time. One of the easiest ways to adjust the strain is with a rope tackle at each of the anchors. Do this by tying a Butterfly Knot in each guyline about 6 to 8 feet from the anchor. Then wrap the running end of the guyline around the forward stake of the anchor and back through the loop in the Butterfly Knot. When rope tackles are tied to all four anchors, gradually tighten the lines. Apply enough strain to each of the guylines to hold the tower firm and in a vertical position. Then tie off the rope tackles and secure the running ends with half hitches.

Test the structure. Before the tower can be put into general use, make a test climb while the safety officer and the whole crew observe all the lashings and anchors to ensure they are all secure.

PROJECT BUILDING: 14' Double Ladder Signal Tower

Because building the 14' Double Ladder Signal Tower affords such a wide range of Scout Pioneering opportunities, it makes a superlative group project for a pioneering merit badge class.

Pioneering Merit Badge Class posing with Their Project at Scout Camp

PIONEERING PROGRAM

A patrol is engaged in planning their approach to completing a pioneering challenge, during the activities segment of the troop meeting.

An established Scout troop is a cyclical enterprise. Within its framework, there is a range of learning experiences and opportunities that repeat themselves—some every year as new members come on board, some on a more regular basis, and some only every so often. Your unit's repertoire of pioneering-based, Scout meeting challenges and favorite pioneering projects can be a regularly-featured part of your ongoing Scouting program.

Staying Focused and Figuring Out the Best Course of Action

As was alluded to in the opening quote of Chapter 4, in Scout Pioneering there needs to be a learning sequence. Scouts can't just jump in and build stuff. They need to go through a readiness process which ideally incorporates actually doing something that reinforces the skills they acquire—something that is engaging and challenging. This is part of a program planning process referred to as a sequential approach.

A SEQUENTIAL APPROACH to program planning is one where gaining specific skills, and then putting them into action, pave the way towards larger experiences that are memorable and rewarding. These larger experiences are ordinarily featured during a "main event" like an outing or special trip. Simply put, with Scout Pioneering, larger experiences can *include* a pioneering project, and sometimes even more than one.

Learn the Skill

Put the Skill Into Action

Use the Skill in a Project

PIONEERING PROGRAM

In sequential programming, the skills acquired and the subsequent activities that are enjoyed during weekly troop meetings are presented in a stepwise progression, like building blocks. The ultimate goal of this sequential approach is to use these building blocks to enable the Scouts to get the most out of larger experiences. These experiences are a culmination of the preceding meetings. In order for the troop's program to be most successful, with the most positive outcomes for the Scouts and their troop, these preceding meetings in themselves should be *filled with fun!*

Scouts cheer on members of their patrol during a lashing skill activity.

As an illustration, what follows is a simple sample of sequential, pioneering programming, featuring a skill and a corresponding activity leading up to a larger experience:

- Meeting 1: Square lashing instruction leading to a **Ladder Building Activity**
- Meeting 2: Tripod lashing instruction leading to an **Everyone on the Tripod** challenge
- Meeting 3: Floor lashing instruction leading to a **Lift Seat Procession**
- Larger Experience: Building a **Chippewa Kitchen**

Relying upon their acquired skills, Scouts build a Chippewa Kitchen..

PIONEERING PROGRAM

Of course, during the outing, the Scouts don't just *build* a Chippewa Kitchen. They use it to prepare fabulous feasts!

Lunch Steamed in Foil Packets and Baked in a Dutch Oven

Scout Pioneering remains a quintessential part of the Scouting movement. It provides a wide range of opportunities for personal growth and has all the qualities that keep Scouts involved and coming back for more. Scouting is a multicolored tapestry of learning and adventure, and Scout Pioneering adds unforgettable shades of challenge and fun.

About the Author

Larry Green is a BSA volunteer who resides in North Myrtle Beach, SC. His memories of Scouting are the source of numerous nostalgic recollections. More than fifty years later, the lasting impact of his experiences as a Scout motivate him to do whatever he can to advance Scouting's mission, and share Scouting's special mystique.

The author on a Double A-Frame Monkey Bridge at Philmont Training Center, during "Planning Programs That Rock," 2016